THE
STRATEGY
BOOK

Create a Strategic Mindset
and Future-Proof Your Business

JOHN HALE

H | HALE
CONSULTING GROUP
VALUE DRIVEN STRATEGIES

www.halecg.com

Published by Hale Consulting Group
267 Grey Street
South Brisbane 4101 Australia
www.halecg.com

Illustrations: Marko Horvat and Megan Taylor
Book Design: Jana Rade
Editing: Samantha Wright

SECOND EDITION
ISBN 978-0-6486590-0-6

A catalogue record for this book is available from the National Library of Australia

By his example, Robert Hale, my father, taught me the satisfaction

of solving problems and teaching others to do the same.

This book is dedicated to him.

CONTENTS

INTRODUCTION

I n thirty-five years of speaking and consulting, I have gained powerful insights from businesses and organizations around the globe. I have met with and listened to some of the most successful consultants, founders and CEOs. I have also sat with some of the least successful. This accumulated experience has encouraged me to share what every leader must cultivate to excel strategically in business.

The word 'strategy' seems to have fallen out of favor in recent years, due to increasing levels of global complexity and digital connectivity, which have brought disruption and an innovative imperative to the world of business strategy. Faith has also waned due to a plethora of bad experiences with superficial and half-baked strategy processes. Yet, a definition of insanity is doing the same thing over and over and expecting a different result. For a better result, strategy is the key. Uncertainty has always been the 'elephant in the room' when formulating a strategy. Using future uncertainty as an excuse to not persevere with strategy is tempting, but foolish. Strategic considerations like Industry Attractiveness, Unfair Advantages, and assembling of the Value Chain are frequently overlooked by today's passionate serial entrepreneurs – to their ultimate disadvantage.

Ultimately, value creation requires discipline. In business, I have witnessed the leader who follows a regular and disciplined planning process, profit in ways that other leaders cannot. Disciplined leaders are those with what I call a Strategic Mindset. An attractive and well-timed business will grow to a certain point without a leader who has cultivated a Strategic Mindset. Charismatic leadership with great ideas can work for a time. However, once disruption occurs, or growth slows, something else is needed to future-proof a business. That something else is a Strategic Mindset. A Strategic Mindset builds a clear, dispassionate and objective view of the emerging future. As a leader, you can create one for yourself with *The Strategy Book*.

FROM DOZENS OF ILLUSTRATIONS, INSIGHTS, AND IDEAS, YOU WILL:

- Appreciate the strengths and limitations of the human brain
- Excel in business by applying the six-step Strategic Mindset Process
- Compile your best ideas and answers to empowering questions
- Better sense your environment and see beyond the next horizon
- Connect with stakeholders to create and capture future value
- Combine focus, speed, and influence to deliver strategy successfully
- Cultivate the ability to manage the present and lead the future

I find education is best driven by action learning – taking actions and reflecting on the results to drive future actions. The lessons gained from life and business, your actions and the actions of others can be invaluable. The Strategy Book draws on experiences from a wide selection of historical settings and industries and advances that have resulted from creative ideas and transformations. There are strategies from my life and work and from companies like Accenture, Adobe, Apple,

Audi, Amazon, BCG, BHP, B&D Doors, Coca-Cola, Eli Lilly, Encyclopedia Britannica, Ford, Google, General Electric, Huawei, Kimberly Clark, IKEA, McDonalds, McKinsey & Company, Microsoft, Monsanto, Motorola, 3M, NASA, Nestle, Nokia, PayPal, PepsiCo, Pixar, Rusty, Shell, Switch, Uber, Velcro, Virgin, Xerox and others.

Other commentators on strategy have at times been opposed to one another, preferring to see the world of strategy through their particular lens. For example, one school of strategic thinking that concerns itself primarily with positioning is often referred to in the literature as "The Positioning School." This School has subgroups loyal to the work of Harvard Business School Professor Michael Porter, while other subgroups are loyal to the Blue Ocean thinking of W. Chan Kim and Renee Mauborgne. Sometimes these subgroups will not acknowledge one another, or when they do, they write and speak out publicly against each other. This commentary highlights a truth about strategy, that 'no one shoe fits' every business, every time.

Schools of thought in the world of strategy have been classified in ten ways.[1] The rational approach to strategy is echoed by five of them; namely the Environmental, Planning, Positioning, Design and Configurations Schools. The intuitive approaches to strategy are echoed by another four; namely the Cognitive, Learning, Cultural and Entrepreneurial Schools. The tenth approach to strategy is tactical. Tacticians within the Power School echo the importance of both rational thinking and human instincts with a strong foundation based in Political Science.

The configuration of activities in The Strategy Book draw upon ideas and questions from all ten schools; however, there is a leaning towards my bias of seeing the strategy creation process as more intuitive than rational and the external world as less predictable. The Strategy Book, therefore, lends better support to the adaptive and emergent approach that today's small business owners and niche players often take with strategy.

The Strategy Book may be less applicable to larger firms, who due to their size, are often more rational and deliberate with strategy and can more clearly see their marketplace. Paradoxically, the small business owner who masters the Strategic Mindset Process will increase their chances of one day, creating a more significant business. Leaders of larger firms that master the Strategic Mindset Process and revisit their Founder's Vision can remain agile, innovative, and likely to learn faster than competitors.

In many ways the game of business is infinite. The future is always inconvenient. However, if you undertake the many activities in The Strategy Book, you will learn how to apply the six-step Strategic Mindset Process and future-proof your business.

CREATE A
STRATEGIC
MINDSET

FRED'S BRAIN

The first Homo Erectus males and females appeared in Africa some 2.5 million years ago[2]. About 2 million years ago, some of these early humans journeyed and settled in the snowy foothills of Europe and Asia. They adapted into more muscular and thicker set northerners called Homo Neanderthalensis. Those who remained in the southern hemisphere became thinner, smarter and more agile. They evolved to become our species, Homo Sapiens.

'Fred' is the name I affectionately give to the Neanderthal species. During my conference talks on strategy, I sometimes produce a life-sized replica of a Neanderthal skull and introduce audiences to 'my old mate Fred.' I then share the final chapter of Fred's journey. Fred's story ends tragically. Some 50,000 years ago, as food became scarce, it is likely that during the summertime, our Homo-Sapien ancestors scaled the Italian Alps to a vista of breath-taking snowy mountain views and subsequently conquered Fred's species. Fred and his kinsfolk appear to have been eradicated by tribes of Sapiens heading northwards and spreading across the Globe.

The success of the Sapiens and the failure of the Neanderthals offer valuable lessons, which we can apply to the competitive and co-operative world of business. As suggested by the shape of their skulls, the Sapiens' brains differ from Neanderthal brains. A Neanderthal skull is elongated and flat, like an NRL or NFL football. A Sapiens skull is rounder, like a basketball and shorter from front to back with a higher and larger forehead. This difference means that proportionally, Fred had more room in his skull for his hindbrain, which accommodated both his parietal and occipital lobes, and less room inside his head for his midbrain, which housed his cerebellum and basal ganglia. Fred's small forehead meant that he had even less room for his frontal cortexes.

Some scientists suggest Fred's large hindbrain offered him excellent night vision and a heightened sensitivity to changes in his immediate environment[3]. Thanks to his large hindbrain, Fred's ability to sense and see was probably superior to ours. When southern tribes of Sapiens invaded, it is likely that Fred saw and sensed their presence first. This ability to sense and see is useful in life and business. Sensing and Seeing are the first two steps of the six-step Strategic Mindset Process.

By contrast, it is possible Fred's smaller frontal cortex and smaller midbrain placed him at a disadvantage, once we Sapiens spotted him. With larger forebrains, our ability to process information, connect and plan was probably superior. If this is true, we could have coordinated our efforts and planned our attacks with greater ease and success than Fred. Connecting and Planning are the third and fourth steps of the six-step Strategic Mindset Process.

Finally, if our midbrains were larger, this would have allowed us to focus and move more strategically and efficiently in the world, due to our cerebellum and basal ganglia's roles in coordination, balance and motivation. At nighttime, Fred could survive better, but when day broke, Fred was easy prey. When compared with Fred, our ability to focus and move strategically is something we likely did better. Focusing and Moving are the fifth and sixth steps of the Strategic Mindset Process. In the end, Fred's brain probably let him down. He could sense and see well, but he may not have been able to connect, plan, focus and move fast enough. To survive and thrive in business, leaders must be proficient in all six-steps.

Leaders can create a Strategic Mindset by following the six-steps:

Step 1. Sense the Environment
Step 2. See Beyond the Next Horizon
Step 3. Connect with Customers and Stakeholders
Step 4. Plan Future Value Chains, Creations and Combinations
Step 5. Focus on a Chosen Target
Step 6. Move Faster with Influence

The six-step Strategic Mindset Process is straight forward and has been crystallized over many years of studying and assisting countless businesses. Creating it has been an amazing journey. Applying it to your business offers you a great opportunity to master your environment, craft strategy deliberately and participate in the new industries of the future.

MY AMAZING JOURNEY

My amazing journey with strategy has been challenging and embarrassing at times. I was not a naturally gifted strategist. As an MBA student, my lowest mark was in the Strategy Unit. My personality is more intuitive than sensory, more extroverted than introverted. When I graduated from Business School, one of my Professors who was an adviser to Boston Consulting Group, offered to help get me a job at BCG. As BCG was one of the top strategy firms globally, I met with them. I soon discovered that BCG's clients were some of the biggest corporations in the world and their client focus seemed to be around efficient leveraged sourcing, synergistic acquisitions, timing deals, large numbers and helping firms to scale up and capture monopolistic-like multiples.

I knew that working as a Strategy Consultant with BCG in a dozen different cities each year would mean I would miss out on seeing my four children grow up. Instead, I started my own consulting practice, where I was soon advising and facilitating strategy. My early attempts at facilitating strategy were tough. I remember one fragmented executive team that looked so worried with my approach it united them against me, but they then worked together in new ways to better own the strategy process. In time, I learnt that creativity, communication, and supporting others were my natural strengths. On the other hand, timing, environmental sensing, and seeing where all the untapped multiples existed, required me to work a little harder.

I tapped into my strengths and used them to keep learning. I kept pushing the boundaries of my understanding. I researched the most intuitive and valuable strategic thinking frameworks I could find. I accepted invitations to teach in business schools, where as a visiting academic, I gained unfettered access to the business school libraries of Harvard, UCLA and others. The more I read, the more I learnt. The more I taught and facilitated strategy, the better I understood how to apply it. Eventually I became proficient in the world of strategy and its contexts, ideas, and tools. At last I was able to drive value for clients in powerful ways. In time, I learnt effective strategy was as much an art as a science – a marriage between analysis and creativity, that draws upon intelligence from many sources.

I may never be the world's best strategist and my success picking stocks is only slightly above average, but I have mastered the creative process and the logic of gaining an advantage. Importantly, I am passionate about helping others. With a strong enough WHY, the HOW will appear[4]. *The Strategy Book* is an outer reflection of my strategy journey. In my consulting practice, strategy remains a continuous journey taken with my clients in three to twelve-month intervals. Each iteration addresses the six-steps. Each step includes activities and ways of thinking that incorporate and creatively combine what I believe, are the best ideas of strategy professionals, military leaders, CEOs, and academics.

If you don't have time to complete a business degree, read hundreds of books, or learn what it takes to be a successful strategy consultant, then *The Strategy Book* will help. If you are a leader who struggles to formulate a strategic future for your firm, try using *The Strategy Book*.

If you are gifted in strategy and timing, you may want to sharpen your process with *The Strategy Book* or perhaps gift it to a creative client or intuitive colleague who you know needs a better strategy.

THE BOOK STRATEGY

Books surrounded me growing up. Our home had rooms neatly filled from floor to ceiling with books of every description. Wherever I looked, there they were: leather-bound Encyclopedia Britannica sets, shelves filled with *National Geographic*, *Life*, *Newsweek* and *Time* magazines, the complete works of Shakespeare and Dickens. I remember titles by Hemingway, Orwell, Scott Fitzgerald, Louis Stevenson, Homer, Plato, Dante, Tolstoy, Goethe, Proust, Chekov, Aesop, Poe, Wilde, Anderson, Joyce and Asimov. I remember titles by Einstein, Knuth and Wirth. Our house was also home to dozens of cold war spy, sci-fi and romance novels.

There were books on poetry, art, music, science, literature, mathematics, computing, philosophy, anthropology, religion, home economics and travel. Swimsuit editions of *Sports Illustrated* or *Wheels* Magazines were nowhere in sight. There was not a single book or magazine about sport, psychology, or business, yet I spent much of my early adult life reading about these subjects – to my parents' amazement.

As you might imagine, in our home, books were a kind of religion and reading was sacred. I rebelled at first, preferring to be outside creating my own world. When I began to read in earnest, I learnt that one must never mark or damage a book. As my reading developed, I found myself wanting to go back for a piece of knowledge, after I had considered it. I discovered bookmarks helped. In high school, sometimes I would bend back the corners of insightful pages. At university, I adapted further and would scribble on the sticky notes I was using for bookmarks. As my library developed and my economic prosperity improved, I wrote notes in the margins of my books and underlined the best ideas.

Occasionally, I visited secondhand book shops, and there I discovered *that people who write inside their books finish reading them.* Research suggests that only half the people who buy a book, actually finish it and if that book is an e-book, only a third will finish it. I would like you to finish this book. I want you to write in it and capture the ideas and strategies that excite and interest you. Most books are one-way monologues. I have designed this book to be a two-way dialogue. A place where you can be informed, inspired, empowered, and entertained, and a place to generate new ideas, create strategies and write them down. To this end, I have designed this book to be a deliberate blend of strategy notes and blank pages.

With this book, I want you to capture and create value. The theme of this book is Creating a Strategic Mindset. I want to share the Strategic Mindset Process and allow you to create your strategic future. One-half of this book contains a collection of frameworks, ideas, processes, stories and suggested activities. The other half comprises blank pages, designed for you to capture your diagnosis, diagrams, deliberations, discoveries and doodles.

Life has taught me that books aid discovery. Non-fiction books are a great source of knowledge while fiction helps us imagine new worlds. Just like a teacher, the right book at the right time brings wisdom. Greek Philosopher Heraclitus said, "No one steps into the same river twice." The next time one steps into a river, it is a different river, and he or she is a different person. Rivers flow, and people grow. I re-read my favourite books. The same text can foster shifting and added perspectives over an entire lifetime. When I re-read a great book, I am a different person. I experience the book differently, and I capture and create new value.

I have attempted to write a book that creates and captures more value than any book I own. I hope this book will be the most valuable book on my shelves, and I hope it will be a useful addition to your shelves as well. Use this book to take notes and develop your ideas and strategies. The goal of this book is that the best ideas in this book will be the ones that you create and write. This book will show you how to Create a Strategic Mindset, using the six steps and then inspire you to develop value-driven strategic futures for your business and your clients.

SENSE THE ENVIRONMENT

SHIPSHAPE

Sensing your Environment

Sensing your environment is the first step of the six-step Strategic Mindset Process. Leaders who rarely sense their environment will not change their course in time to save their ship. Like a Neanderthal who sleeps in the fork of a tree during the day, they are asking for trouble! Because our brains like to take shortcuts, a firm's inside view of its internal and external environments, once established, usually shapes biased beliefs about both the internal and external environment for years or even decades to come.

When I board a client ship, I ask to see their financial statements for the last three years, so I can get a sense of their internal and external environment. I make a note of the current economic tides. A rising sea lifts the biggest boats the best. In tough economic times, with shallow water, careless big boats easily run aground. I also complete a cultural audit via employee interviews. I examine their mission, claim to fame and business model to see how valuable and scalable it is. As I work with a client, I gauge their leadership abilities and together we aim to gain a sense of what is happening externally. I use the analogy of a ship and its crew on the ocean. There is no point weighing anchor and setting a new course, without an up-to-date sense of both the internal and external environments.

In assessing the internal environment, I am interested in the overall strength of their ship. First up, I note investment in Research and Development. The more intelligent R&D being done, the sturdier the ship. Second, I examine the wisdom of the captain and officers. Are they seasoned and seaworthy? What have they learnt along the way? Third, I consider financial ratios, like short-term liquidity and long-term solvency. Are there enough resources to support a healthy continuation of the existing strategy or a change in policy? Finally, I assess the client's capabilities, organizational structure, systems and the crew. Some crew members are mutineers. Some crews fight. Others are there for a free ride. Some jump ship at the first sign of trouble. The best crews trust their captain, the ship's officers, and other crew members.

The other environment that needs assessing is the external one. How attractive, changeable, and predictable is it?

The first step is to understand the attractiveness of the industry the business operates in. We typically assess six forces at work in the industry, their intensity and their impact on profits. We look at the color of the 'ocean' they are in. A Blue Ocean[5] is ideal. A red ocean, less so. A Blue Ocean is an uncontested and attractive new market with fresh demand, where a ship can chart its course freely. A red ocean is an existing saturated and unattractive industry filled with hungry competitors.

The second step is to understand market changeability – by measuring how adaptable customers are to change. BCG's *Strategy Palette* provides a helpful framework for understanding change, by examining factors like industry harshness, malleability and unpredictability[6].

Assessing industry predictability is our third step. Trade winds are good. New industries enjoy fair winds. Growing industries enjoy trade winds and smooth sailing. Mature industries experience crosswinds and tailwinds. Industries in decline are predictable, with headwinds and reducing fortunes. For many industries, unpredictability is increasing in the era of advancing digital innovation. With close to 100% of people in the developed world and 50% of people in the developing world with Internet access, business sailing ships are converting into spaceships, that are trading more and more in the digital atmosphere.

Evolving businesses may operate with fewer crew members and rely less on traditional business relationships, resources and methods. Technologies like Robotics, Artificial Intelligence (AI), Advanced Cognition Processes, Cloud, Big Data, Blockchain and the Internet of Things have changed the picture and disrupted traditional players. For example, at the end of the nineteenth century the Lumière brothers invented Cinema. Television arrived by the 1930s. Cable TV entered in the 1960s. Video arrived in the 1970s. DVDs in the mid-1980s. On Demand by the 2000s. Live Streaming in the mid to late-2000s and interactive customisable movies with virtual reality headsets, gloves and suits in the 2020s.

In the 1970's, Michael Porter studied hundreds of businesses. He realized that over time Industry Attractiveness changed and the attractiveness of an industry could be determined by examining six industry forces[7]. The sum of customer power, supplier power, threat of new entrants, threat of substitutes, degree of rivalry and complementary player effects reveal the likely profitability of an industry. Use Michael Porter's model to assess the prevailing profitability of your industry.

ACTIVITY 1.1
INDUSTRY ATTRACTIVENESS

1. On the blank pages opposite, write down a description of your Industry. For example, Legal Services, Cloud Computing, Real Estate, Domestic Robotics, Retail Fashion, Beauty, Café, Homewares, Software Development, Health, Mining, Education, Manufacturing, etc.

2. Jot down the Customers or Clients that regularly buy from your Industry. For example, European consumers represent one-tenth of the world population, yet they account for one-third of sales in the Global Haircare Industry. Decide if the bargaining power of customers (Customer Power) is low, moderate, or high.

3. Make a list of the major Suppliers to your Industry. For example, the Café Industry may rely on Suppliers of retail spaces, chefs, baristas, insurance, equipment, food, beverages and coffee. Decide if the bargaining power of suppliers (Supplier Power) is low, moderate, or high.

4. Assess the Threat of New Entrants to your Industry by jotting down their likely barriers to entry. For example, high-cost barriers for entry to the Industry; existing customers' perceived costs of switching their purchasing to a New Entrant; government policies; existing intellectual property (IP) and the threat of retaliation by incumbents, such as yourself. Decide if the Threat of New Entrants is low, moderate, or high.

5. Make a list of products and services that are Substitutes for what you produce. For example, in the Automotive Industry, the list of possible Substitutes includes public transport, rideshare and electric scooters. Decide if the Threat of Substitutes is low, moderate, or high.

6. Make a list of rival players, who compete against you and each other for customers and market share. Decide if the Degree of Rivalry in your Industry is low, moderate, or high.

7. Consider related industries. Complementary players are firms in nearby industries with activities that complement your Industry. For example, when large firms behave unethically and more customers sue them, this increased litigation activity benefits the Legal Profession. Decide if the Benefits from Complementary Players in your industry are low, moderate, or high.

    Some industries are attractive, with lots of green lights. For example, at the time of writing, Dentists enjoy 20% profit margins with friendly trade winds. For Dentists, Customer Power, Threat of Substitutes, Threat of New Entrants, Degree of Rivalry are all low, with Supplier Power being high and Benefits from Complementary Players being moderate. Other industries are less attractive, with more yellow and red lights. For example, Airlines have profit margins of around 5% with plenty of crosswinds. For Airlines, Supplier Power, Customer Power, Threat of Substitutes, Threat of New Entrants and Degree of Rivalry are all moderate or high, with Benefits from Complementary Players being only moderate.

8. Review your answers and decide how attractive your industry is, overall. Is the **Overall Industry Attractiveness** low, moderate, or high? How easy are your customers to reach? What is the average net profit across your industry? Where are the most favorable winds to be found? For example, software development is usually much more attractive than hardware manufacturing. Will digital innovation make your Industry more or less attractive in the future?

Reflect on your answers. If the attractiveness of your industry is low, with recessionary economic or industry trends that could drive profitability down further, you may not expect your business to survive in its current form. If so, consider withdrawing and conserving cash for a better game than the one you are in. Escalation of commitment and doubling down on a failing strategy is all too common and misguided. If you continue, keep watching your customer service quality, your return on investment and your opportunity costs. Try to avoid any false pride or attachment bias toward sunk costs. Also consider recurring revenue streams like subscriptions and maintenance contracts alongside the failure of a one-off project or declining product sales.

CUSTOMER BARGAINING POWER
— H / M / L

SUPPLIER BARGAINING POWER
— H / M / L

THREAT OF NEW ENTRANTS
— H / M / L

THREAT OF SUBSTITUTES
— H / M / L

DEGREE OF RIVALRY
— H / M / L

BENEFITS FROM COMPLEMENTS
— L / M / H

OVERALL INDUSTRY ATTRACTIVENESS
— L / M / H

STEP ONE: SENSE THE ENVIRONMENT

"The world we live in is vastly different from the world we think we live in."

Nassim Nicholas Taleb

STEP ONE: SENSE THE ENVIRONMENT

RHYTHMS

Staying in tune

When business leaders slow down, sense their environment, and tune in, they can decide whether to advance, keep listening or withdraw. If a business regularly senses how favorable and attractive conditions are becoming, decisions about survival, future strategy and actions are much more straightforward and accurate. Encyclopedia Britannica is a classic example of a legacy business that did not look in the rear-view mirror to see what was about to overtake them. Encyclopedia Britannica became out of tune with its marketplace. A thirty-two-volume Encyclopedia Britannica set was selling for two-thousand dollars, at a time when digital innovation occurred in the Knowledge Reference Industry. At that time New Entrants were selling the same information on CD-ROM for two-hundred dollars.

Today, a Substitute like Wikipedia offers one-hundred times more information for a voluntary donation, and Google Search is free. There is a rhythm a business must have to survive and thrive. Every successful leader learns to drive a business as we drive a car. As the terrain changes, drivers and leaders must adapt to changing conditions. There is a pattern of tuning in, that successful drivers and leaders must learn.

Recently, Ari, one of my son's sixteen-year-old friends, asked if he could drive us to our destination. Ari put his learner plates on my car and started driving. Ari seemed confident and kept a safe distance from the traffic in front and beside us. I complimented Ari on his driving.

After driving for a while on a long stretch of road, I asked Ari to tell me without looking in his mirrors, what traffic was behind him. He shared that he had no clue and hardly ever looked behind. We then talked about the importance for a driver to be constantly in tune with their surrounding environment to survive on the road. Ari agreed that knowing what traffic was behind, in front, and beside us, made sense. The best leaders also stay in tune.

If you are already in tune, summarizing shifting industry patterns may be quite easy. An *in-tune business* will understand changes in attractiveness and demand within their industry as well as its current growth rate. A *well-tuned* business will be an in-tune business which also understands the recent shifts in products, sales channels and market segments. A *finely tuned* business will be a well-tuned business that also understands how the needs and preferences of customers are changing and the future critical success factors that need to be met, including the importance of competitor moves, price and the future impact of significant new technologies.

ACTIVITY 1.2
CLAIM TO FAME

1. Define your **Claim to Fame**. Encyclopedia Britannica's Claim to Fame was that it was the longest-serving and most trusted general knowledge English-language encyclopedia. Your Claim to

Fame could reflect your Founder's Vision, your business intent, elevator statement or Ideal Customer definition. For example, the 'Big Australian' mining company BHP had founders renowned for 'thinking big'. BHP's Claim to Fame is that it owns and operates large, long-life, low-cost, expandable, upstream assets diversified by commodity, geography, and market.

2.   How do your customers and the marketplace perceive you? What lasting and valuable contribution does your business or firm make to the world? On the blank pages opposite write down your Claim to Fame. Consider your respective competitors' Claims to Fame. How is your Claim to Fame really that different from theirs? In the end, the points of difference you identify and embody may make a world of difference.

3.   Consider what it takes to be really successful in your Industry. For example, if you own a Gym which operates in the Fitness Industry, you might come up with the following six Critical Success Factors: 1. Sound financial management; 2. High levels of customer service; 3. Appealing workout and training spaces with modern equipment; 4. Safe, social and educational training programs and classes; 5. Membership pricing that aligns with a range of client preferences; 6. Clean change and shower facilities. On the blank pages opposite, list the **Critical Success Factors** for any business in your industry – write out the three to six most important things you must do well for your business to thrive?

4.   To keep your business finely tuned, knowing your Claim to Fame and understanding the Industry Attractiveness and Critical Success

Factors as the terrain changes, will require regular review. On the blank pages opposite, write down how regularly your business will do this and who will be involved. For a small business, this could be your peers. For a mature or established business, this may involve board members and the senior leadership team.

CLAIM TO FAME

1. _____ 4. _____

2. _____ 5. _____

3. _____ 6. _____

STEP ONE: SENSE THE ENVIRONMENT

"Strategy has not been tried and found lacking.
Strategy has been found onerous and left untried."

John Hale

KEEP SENSING

The Second Wave

Many years ago, my friend Mario and I used to follow the long lonely roads out west across Australia. We would visit and advise regional and remote local government councils and communities on strategy and risk. At sunset, we saw many kangaroos and sensed that thousands of roos were on the move. We tuned in and moved at a steady pace to avoid collisions in this environment. The less predictable and more dangerous threat were emus. When we saw an emu, we slowed right down, until we spied the second emu. These ostrich-like birds travel in pairs, often roaming 150m apart. If an emu raced across the road in front of us, there was every chance that a few seconds later, out of nowhere, the second emu would speed past the front of our car to be with its mate.

With each new wave of technology, a second and far more significant wave may follow. People often overestimate the initial impact of new technology and underestimate its influence in the long run. Mario and I were very cautious of the emus we could see. Eventually, we sensed it would be the emu we couldn't see that could have the most significant impact.

In the four years that followed the 2014 hype about self-driving cars, I sensed a lot of talk, which has now fallen away. Many overestimated the initial impact of self-driving cars, believing they would take over the world by 2020. Driverless vehicles have taken much longer to gain acceptance. However, their impact on society will be enormous. We will see fewer drivers in highway lanes, with some vehicles converting into drones and travelling in skyway lanes. Cars are making way for new transport services, with fewer road fatalities.

In Australia, a few years ago, waves of global auto giants tested their autonomous cars out west – they now design them to account for roos that jump randomly. I wonder how it will all go in the long run? When I go riding out west on my motorbike, I have learnt to sense trouble one or two corners ahead of time. I can usually sense a nearby roo. When the roo jumps out in front of me, I have learnt to adapt to their unpredictable last-second random moves. I brake smoothly and keep myself on a collision path with the roo. If I swerve to avoid the roo, there is a 50% chance the roo will jump at the last minute and hit me. If I aim for the roo, at the last minute, there is a 50% chance the roo will jump left and a 50% chance the roo will jump right. By slowing and aiming straight for the roo, the chance I will actually hit the roo is close to zero. In the unlikely event that the roo freezes, it is still safer for me to run over a stationary roo, that hit a moving one!

As auto giants fine-tune the algorithm that predicts kangaroos, the emu that follows and the gravity-assisted drone collision fallout from the skyways, things are becoming very different. As industries become different and customers adapt, businesses must understand both factors.

ACTIVITY 1.3
STRATEGIC APPROACH

1. Tune into the industry in which you operate. How **Predictable** is your industry? On the blank pages opposite, make a list of all the predictable things about your industry that don't seem to be changing. Is your industry highly predictable or more unpredictable? Predictable industries include soft drinks, transport logistics and mortgage finance; there is little change afoot. Less predictable industries include ride services, biotechnology and online retail shopping; here it may be hard to predict who will be the next round of winners. For example, is the effect of digital innovation predictable in your industry? When will it change things? What will its impact be? If it has not happened already, will mainstream manufacturing technologies like 3D printing, robotics and AI mean your industry eventually becomes a service industry? Not all new technologies are disruptive. A disruptive technology is one that upsets existing product configurations or value chain activities in ways that change the level of competitive advantage between firms.

2. Consider how **Adaptable** customers are in your industry. Are customers in your industry adaptable and easily swayed by new trends? Are they constantly on the lookout for new products or services? For example, there are lots of customer-driven changes in alternative healthcare, dietary products and holiday travel packages; or are customer preferences in your industry relatively stable, for example, there are few customer-driven changes in automobiles, office supplies, and commercial banking.

Reflect on your answers. If your market is predictable and customers are slow to adapt, then continuing to grow the size of your existing customer base makes sense – keep penetrating your existing markets with a **Market Approach**. The more customers you have, the higher your revenue to costs ratio should be. For example, online shopping is predictable and not going away. Online customers were once slow to adapt and required high levels of trust. Trusted players like Amazon understood this and kept developing their existing markets, as each day went by.

If your market is predictable and customers are quite willing and able to adapt, then taking a more **Visionary Approach** may be prudent. If your business aligns well with the evolving needs of customers, then if you plan and build something different and even better, they will likely come along. With their visionary and well-timed approach, Apple seemed to understand what customers needed when they introduced their iPods, iPhones, iPads and Apple Watches.

If your market seems to be in flux and highly unpredictable, you may have little power to change ingrained customer preferences. If so, then taking an **Agile Approach** makes sense. Innovation and repeated experimentation may allow you to stumble upon the right product or service, at least for a time. Big Pharmaceutical companies like Pfizer and Eli Lilly stay agile by routinely investing 15% to 25% of their sales revenue in R&D. Google, Microsoft and Adobe invest around 10%. Legendary entrepreneur, Richard Branson, experimented a great deal. Many of his Virgin branded experiments were not scalable, but a few like Virgin Mobile, Virgin Megastore, Virgin Money, and Virgin Airlines scaled well in the market for a time.

Another scenario is where your market is highly unpredictable, but customers are adaptable. Here joint partnerships with other players and influential stakeholders make for a **Partnering Approach** that helps to create new standards in the industry. Uber teamed up with independent drivers and riders as well as popular restaurants to create new levels of customer service and new ways of getting people and their meals around. Research shows ninety-five percent of businesses fail within ten years[8]. Over time, your firm's ability to pivot and change its strategic direction, from say an Agile Approach to a Visionary Approach, or from a Market Approach to a Partnering Approach, may dramatically increase your chances of finishing in the winning five percent.

Where you choose to play and which customers you serve will not change overnight, but in time, to survive and thrive, strategic adjustments will always be needed.

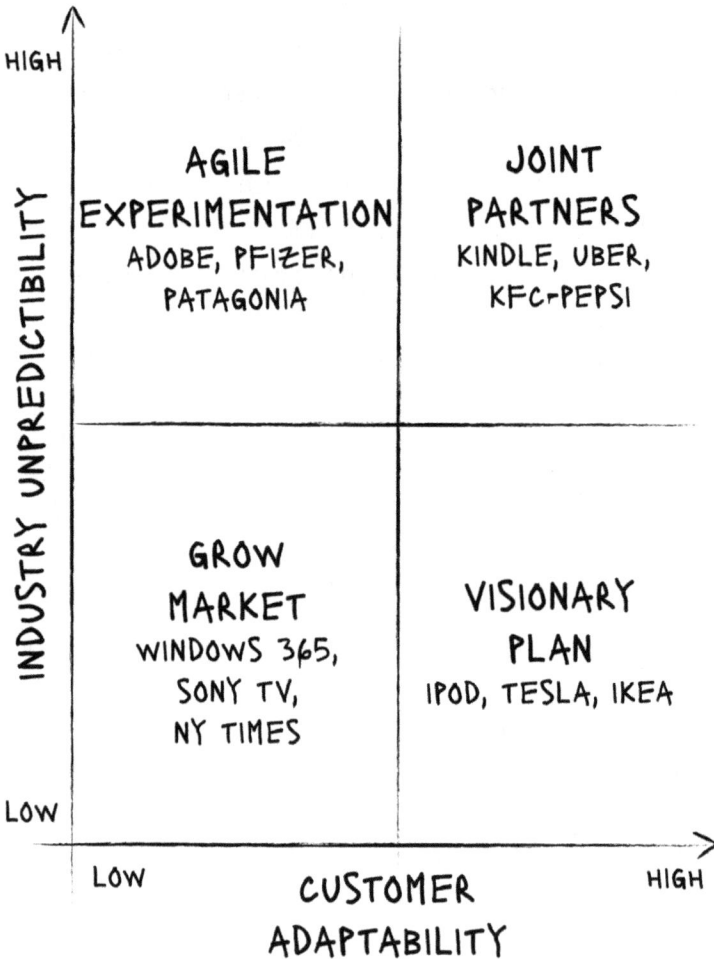

HIGH

INDUSTRY UNPREDICTIBILITY

AGILE EXPERIMENTATION
ADOBE, PFIZER, PATAGONIA

JOINT PARTNERS
KINDLE, UBER, KFC-PEPSI

GROW MARKET
WINDOWS 365, SONY TV, NY TIMES

VISIONARY PLAN
IPOD, TESLA, IKEA

LOW

LOW

CUSTOMER ADAPTABILITY

HIGH

"Your environment dictates your approach to strategy."

Martin Reeves

SEE BEYOND THE NEXT HORIZON

THE NEXT HORIZON

Who will cut your Lunch?

The second step of the six-step Strategic Mindset Process is to see beyond the next horizon. Our collective future will continue to be shaped by an increasingly hyperconnected internet, spectacular advances in software intelligence, big data and virtually limitless computing power. These advances have created new levels of uncertainty and volatility, the likes of which the world has never seen. Are businesses now more fragile than ever? At times, one or two false moves can be deadly. Smart moves can produce profitable results.

One hundred and fifty years ago, following the Industrial Revolution, to have a successful business, one only needed to rent a shopfront next to the others, collect fresh produce from the local farmers and mill, bake and cook to sell prepared food for a profit – a tidy little business, which in time, could be handed down to one's children. There seemed to be few changes afoot, and a business owner needed no law degree or much of a strategy. Things seemed stable, to a point. However, as author, former trader and risk analyst, Nassim Nicholas Taleb asserts, there is no long-term stability without short-term volatility[9].

Ironically, our ability to respond to increasing levels of volatility, uncertainty, complexity and ambiguity (VUCA) has made many modern businesses stronger, more stable and better able to navigate the horizon. For example, volatility has exposed flaws in less strategically apt businesses that were fragile. In the late 1940s, Richard and Maurice McDonald created the

Speedee Service System of burger production, that delivered 'just in time' meals and set new standards for fast food service.

Speedee was a good strategy and endowed the McDonald brothers with an unfair advantage over other players. However, Richard and Maurice were fragile. Their decision to take on franchise businessman Ray Kroc as a business partner introduced a new volatility, which exposed their weaknesses. Ray's experience as a travelling salesman, his adventurous spirit and repeated ability to keep growing in the face of volatility, uncertainty, complexity and ambiguity allowed Ray to take over McDonalds and drive the McDonalds brothers out.

Today, VUCA is still with us. That self-driving scooter coming around the next corner could be Uber Eats driving a Big Mac and Fries somewhere fast. Many people are still making food choices that are quicker and cheaper. Uber entered with a good strategy. Uber Eats removed the hassle of having to drive, park, collect dinner and wait for a table at a favorite city restaurant. Uber reminds us how volatile a market can become. We must keep our eyes open and keep fostering our ability to see over the next horizon.

Everything we once used to build our business with could one day evaporate before our eyes. Richard and Maurice McDonald provide a good example. The Global Financial Crisis and the Pandemic provide others. A century ago, the pattern of shopping for food seemed stable and sure. Today our refrigerators are ordering the food, and our robotic kitchens are preparing just in time meals from any recipe that our virtual assistants can find on the internet. In time, both Uber Eats and McDonalds, as we know them, could dissipate and disappear.

ACTIVITY 2.1
VALUE BUILDING

1. On the blank pages opposite, jot down a list of your firm's value-creating assets and resources, such as plant, equipment, artificial intelligence systems, intellectual property, cash reserves, forward contracts and people, that make up your **Core Businesses**. To remain successful, it makes sense to manage your Core Businesses in ways that build value and maximize asset performance, profits, and cash. Your firm's core businesses make up what is often called your realized strategy. Your firm may have reached this point as the result of a previous deliberate strategy or an emergent strategy – where the path to follow presented itself organically.

   McKinsey & Company often call a firm's core business Horizon One as part of their Three Horizons of Growth model. As we have just seen, Horizon One is about **Value Building** within the existing Core Business. Horizon Two is about **Value Migration**, using entrepreneurial and emerging opportunities, which often require placing bets with significant investment to realize the profits associated with them. Finally, Horizon Three is about **Value Exploration**. Here options generated result from small investments in new ideas, R&D and pilot programs. Value Migration and Value Exploration are often the source of intended strategy, which may ultimately be unrealized, or form part of a firm's realized strategy. Firms that survive and thrive have business leaders who balance their energy and attention across all three horizons concurrently.

Leaders who can manage the present and lead the future are rare and valuable.

2. On the blank pages opposite, besides your firm's list of Core Businesses, write down all the ways you might **build increased levels of asset performance, profitability, and cash flow.** For example, is it cheaper to sell physical assets and lease them back? What range of improvable factors have the greatest impact on customer satisfaction? If you have a B2B business, can you offer buyers a discount for early payment and ask suppliers for extended payment terms in return for your loyalty?

HORIZON ONE

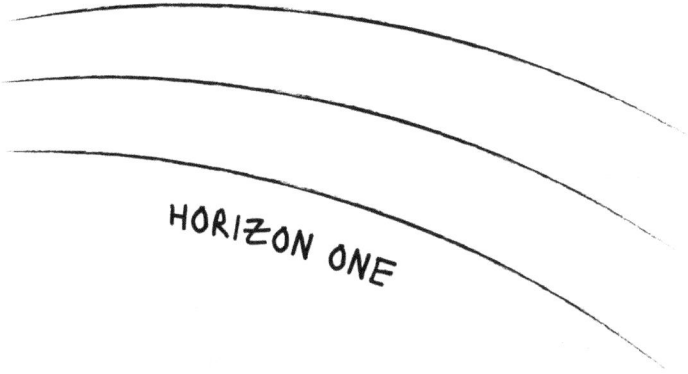

CORE BUSINESS

"I am rare, and there is value in all rarity; therefore, I am valuable."

Og Mandino

PLAY THE ODDS

Think like 'a Bookie'

Good timing is often needed for success. Luck can play an important part in the outcome of strategy. At times, after all the right data has been collected and market intelligence is understood, risks still exist. Businesses must place bets. I grew up in the South Pacific, the United States and Australia. Today, Australian casinos are busy with mostly Asian gamblers. In the United States, people gamble on lots of things, including sport and the stock market. When I was a teenager, Australia was very much a horse and dog racing culture. At the racetrack, a 'bookie' was the person who picked the odds of a horse or dog winning or placing and taking people's bets. At school, some students placed bets amongst themselves on horse and greyhound races.

A family friend, Alex, who was a few years older than me, would take horse bets from other students on the 'Melbourne Cup', which is the largest annual horse race in Australia. Alex was bright and had come up with a good set of odds. Odds he hoped would give him a nice profit. When race day arrived, his father, Joe, who had recently discovered Alex's illegal activity, demanded that he see all the bets. Upon examination, Joe realized that if all the horses ran to form, his son would do very well. However, if any two of the favorite horses stumbled or finished in the back of the field, the bets Alex would have to honor would leave him short!

Joe took Alex to the track to place some bets against the bets his son had collected. They created a hedge, that covered any major downside risks. It was a good strategy. If the favorites did well, Alex would do well. If the favorites raced poorly, Alex could also do well. Joe helped Alex balance his exposure. The race produced mixed results. In his first and last time as an illegal bookie, Alex did well. Odds exist in life and business as well. To ensure success, companies must invest in promising events with big payoffs and hopefully scale them. A business also must balance its bets by staying mindful of unlikely events that would have catastrophic consequences and develop hedge strategies as cover.

A few years later, Alex, in an odd turn of events, became a spiritual seeker and went to live in a Buddhist Monastery. I sense that Alex realized somewhere along the way, his soul could be at risk. He may have felt that the promise and probability of him making lots of money might not bring him true happiness. For Alex, a life unexamined spiritually might carry this downside risk. One he was not prepared to take. Perhaps he had learnt to play the odds and hedge his bets in a more balanced way.

ACTIVITY 2.2
HEDGING BETS

1. Horizon Two is about **Value Migration.** Being entrepreneurial, leveraging emerging opportunities and converting weaknesses into strengths may require a business to place bets on what they

expect will be profitable. On the blank pages opposite, write down a list of emerging opportunities and perceived weaknesses for your business. Revisit your **Claim to Fame** and the **Critical Success Factors** for your Industry, both now and moving forward. Draw a circle around those opportunities that align best with your Claim to Fame and help you better meet the Critical Success Factors for your Industry. Also note which Critical Success Factors you perform weakest on.

2. For a few minutes, revisit the idea of **VUCA** for your industry. On the blank pages opposite, write a list of at least five unlikely future events, that could be catastrophic to your business. These could be low probability but highly dangerous threats from a competitor.

3. Other unlikely future events may simply be game changers for all players. Once your list is complete, ask a colleague to review your list and come up with some ideas and options for limiting your exposure, should these unlikely events materialize!

4. Come up with a way to **play the odds**. Consider giving no more than 90% of your energy and resources to what seems to be the best current and future bets for your business. Now consider allocating no less than 10% of your future energy and resources to cover any downsides. Hedge your bets. Ensure you have something in place that deals with and capitalizes on highly unlikely situations, that could be catastrophic, if not addressed ahead of time. Write down what catastrophe looks like. Note down the percentage of your firm's resources that could be used to hedge against it. Describe

ways your business could capitalize on catastrophic events and what moves you plan to make.

5. A great way to hedge your bets in the technology space, migrate value into your business and avoid the shocks associated with digital disruption is to take an **incremental approach with AI and technology adoption**. Each month or each quarter, somewhere in the business, perhaps in design, innovation, manufacturing, distribution, cyber protection, augmenting human capabilities, or the current business model, new technology is implemented in some way. It may be quite easy to keep migrating automation, advanced cognition and cyber intelligence into your business, if it is done regularly.

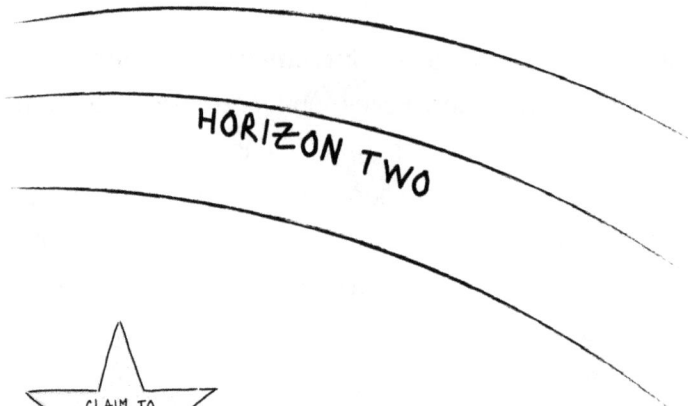

CLAIM TO
FAME

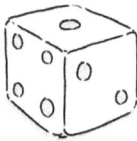

_____

_____

_____

_____

_____

"The problem with the future is that it is different, if you are unable to think differently, the future will always arrive as a surprise."

Gary Hamel

THREE-EYED RAVENS

Learn to See

Many possible and parallel futures exist. Indigenous people were deeply connected with their environment and understood the power of intention. In the wilderness, threats to survival loomed large. Any noise attracted unwanted attention. Indigenous people watched more and spoke less. When men spoke, their word was law. They listened to birds and animals and watched nature to read the future. Today, progress has made us lazy. Foresight has been replaced by our insatiable minds and their constant chatter. As a talking bird, the raven had mythical status. Like a coyote, the raven became a mediator between current and future worlds. In the HBO series, Game of Thrones, when Brandon Stark becomes the Three-Eyed Raven, he can see possible futures.

In business, timing can be the most crucial determinant of success. Seeing possible futures, before they arrive, places a business in the best position to choose between options. As we have seen, McKinsey and Company's Three Horizons for Growth Framework[10] offers us a way to understand both current and future options for value-driven growth. Value Building for one's business means continuously improving what is currently done and scaling it at the right time in ways that maximize Return on Investment (ROI). However, one also must see further. Before business models reach their use-by dates, innovative ideas are required to see what the business can become. This second way of seeing is via

Value Migration. Value Migration is accelerating qualified value-driven future ideas and functioning prototypes towards the present.

A future business iteration might include new services, enhanced products, untapped markets, or movement along the Industry Value Chain. For example, a business may migrate backwards into manufacturing or migrate forward into retail stores. Deciding between Value Migration options that are aligned with the Claim to Fame and the Industry's Critical Success Factors may also require a Net Present Value (NPV) calculation, using the expected future cash flows and required rates of return for each opportunity.

Beyond Value Building and Value Migration is a vast unknown horizon. This is a world of loose and free Value Exploration, beyond the confines and conditioned mindsets of regular business. Value Exploration is the world of future options, expected probability calculations, uncertainty and disruptive innovation. It is the domain of the Three-Eyed Raven, the Serial Entrepreneur and the Lean Startup. Leaders support Value Exploration when they cultivate their intuitive sixth sense and learn to trust their gut.

Another way is when employees are allowed or, even better, paid to tinker and incur small financial losses. Let loose to 'bootleg', creative employees and agile teams can often stumble on something rather significant. 3M was once a failed quarry mining business. Coca-Cola started as a pharmaceutical. Apple made circuit boards for home computer builders. Each was prepared to re-imagine their business, based on the value of the options they were exploring.

Beyond the next horizon are options. Options are often superior to strategies. Many firms create strategic plans based on fixed mindsets that are built on pre-approved budgets and past patterns. These strategic plans rarely have any teeth. Other firms include their values, vision, mission and a collection of beautiful images in their strategic plan. These plans serve as a behavioral change tool or marketing and may not address the real-world choices needed. In my strategy conversations with frustrated CEOs, I see that middle managers two or three layers down often push back against any new strategy. Another three layers further down, those staff closest to customers roll their eyes with blank faces and complain to customers that the CEO and senior management are out of touch with customer needs. On a long enough timeline, the CEO is not the most important. The 'customer is king' and regularly exploring the world through their eyes can be invaluable.

ACTIVITY 2.3
VALUE EXPLORATION

1. On the blank pages opposite complete a traditional SWOT analysis[11] for your firm. Draw a 2 x 2 table containing four boxes or cells. Write four headings; one in each cell: '(our) Strengths', '(our) Weaknesses', 'Opportunities (we have)' and 'Threats (from outside the business)'. Write down a list of your thoughts and ideas about your business under each heading.

2. Any matching items you listed under **Threats** and **Weaknesses** are high priority issues that represent big risks to your firm if not addressed. Any matching items you listed under **Opportunities** and **Strengths** are useful to consider for Value Building your business and some may be good choices for Value Migration. Look at all your **Threats** – consider these when hedging your bets. Redo the SWOT analysis with the word **Options** instead of Opportunities. Options are inherently strategic and come with known choices. Opportunities are more vague or general by nature. When Steve Jobs returned to Apple, he gave himself two options; one option was to build the biggest computer in the world and rent space on it; the other option was to build small personal devices and sell them to everybody. If you gave yourself a choice of two options for future Value Exploration, jot down what they would be. Which option offers customers the greatest value?

3. On the blank pages opposite, write down the names and roles of the people responsible for developing strategy in your firm. If your firm is large, how are responsibilities shared? Then consider the following: If you are a CEO or business owner, the best use of your time may be **meeting with customers and exploring the world of longer horizon futures and options** for the business. If this is true, see if you can delegate the task of migrating the shorter horizon futures for the business to your CFO or Financial Controller. Once you, your CFO and HRM have agreed on the best bets for migration, delegate building these and increasing the overall return on investment to your COO or Operations Manager. Delegation like this maximizes your time and opportunity as a CEO to explore while leaving the migration and building to others.

HORIZON THREE

S	W
OPPORTUNITIES	T

S	W
OPTIONS	T

"For me, it is always important that I go through all the possible options for a decision."

Angela Merkel

CONNECT WITH CUSTOMERS & STAKEHOLDERS

DIALOGUE

While Walking About

By now, you may have a sense that strategy is not an event or an annual offsite. Strategy is an ongoing dialogue. Dialogue happens when we allow others the chance to shift our view of the world. Effective dialogues are an ongoing source of strategic insight. To dialogue effectively, we first must connect. The third step in the six-step Strategic Mindset Process is to connect with customers and stakeholders. Without connecting, leaders restrict their world views and allow themselves to make decisions in a vacuum. A leader may feel safe or even powerful isolated from the real world, but this sense of safety and power is not real – the leader becomes exposed, ignorant, and powerless. On the other hand, connected leaders may choose to answer their own phone and use it to make follow-up calls to customers. Leaders who develop powerful interpersonal relationships based on trust and friendship with colleagues, co-workers, customers and suppliers are rare. Leaders who encourage their organization to do the same create unfair firmwide advantages, which other less connected leaders and firms cannot imitate.

When leaders dialogue, they gain important insights. Until 2000, Korean Air had more crashes than almost any other airline. Korean Air co-pilots, due to a culture of deferring to their elders, contributed to fatal decision making inside the cockpit[12]. Black box recordings from crash wreckages revealed that when Korean co-pilots had offered up timely suggestions for avoiding catastrophe, senior pilots would take offence at such impertinence and fail to act, on principle!

Only humility by the senior pilots to allow dialogue could have prevented the crashes. The same is true for business leaders. Steve Jobs, on his return to Apple, was asked about his hiring practices. Steve humbly replied that he wanted to hire the smartest people so they could tell him what to do. In true Socratic style, Steve dialogued intensely with everyone. When dialoguing with a friend, Steve discovered that despite dozens of Apple models there was no clear answer to which computer was right for his friend. Soon thereafter, in a product meeting, Steve used what this customer taught him to help people choose an Apple Computer that was right for them[13]. Apple eliminated over half of its products and Steve told his team: 'We only need to learn two answers from customers buying an Apple Computer: Are you a professional user or an everyday user? Do you want a desktop or a portable?'

Steve went further at Apple, taking the lessons learnt from the dialogue friendly design of workspaces at Pixar. At Pixar they said, "Art is a team sport."[14] By creating connecting centralised spaces, which employees would have to walk through during the day for coffee, snacks and meetings, Steve forced his leaders and teams to connect with each other. Apple employees constantly passed ideas in passing, rather than staying locked away all day in their individual departments. Thanks to Steve's dialoguing, Apple transformed its level of customer intimacy from being a *Product Provider* with a network of resellers to *Selling the Benefits* directly via Apple Stores. Apple engaged in *Two-way Relationships* with customers, which eventually led to a community of *Alliance Partners,* via its App Store and third-party add-ons.

The best leaders engage in dialogue. They lead by walking about. They connect humbly with stakeholders and customers alike. They fearlessly pursue the most unpleasant truths. They seek the knowledge that others don't even know they have inside themselves. They suspend judgement, foster curiosity and foster the dialogues, rather than monologues, which push people for real insights, creative ideas, and value-driven alliances. They foster ongoing connections with stakeholders and customers for the life of their leadership.

ACTIVITY 3.1
STAKEHOLDERS AND CUSTOMERS

1. On the blank pages opposite create a list of all your **Stakeholders**: downstream customers, distributors, end users, owners, shareholders, regulators, upstream suppliers, competitors, complementary players and any others you can think of. For each customer group jot down their respective wants, needs and motivations. Note each stakeholder's respective level of interest in the strategy creation process as well as their ability to affect its success or otherwise. Often stakeholders closest to the customer are full of ideas and understanding, yet paradoxically, those furthest from the customer can hold the most power to change the strategy[15]. How well do you really know each stakeholder group? Really? Score yourself out of ten for each group on how well you know them.

2. Next time you meet your **Customer**, suspend judgement about who they are and what they need. Stay curious. They have a gift inside you will hear if you stay quiet. What are they focused on at the moment? What challenges are they facing? What must they do more of? What must they do less of? If you can elicit a customer's answers to these four questions, you will have a dialogue that is going places. On the blank pages opposite, write the names of three types of customers you will meet with sometime this month to dialogue with. Consider the relationship your firm has with each. Are your customers early-adopters, mainstream users or late to adopt? Decide if they come to you, or do you chase them, or do they walk away. Consider choosing a highly satisfied customer or 'raving fan', a somewhat satisfied customer and a highly dissatisfied ex-customer or 'terrorist'.

3. In terms of **Customer Intimacy**, are you simply a *Product Provider*? If so, how might you better *Sell the Benefits*, build better *Two-way Relationships* with customers and perhaps attract complementary *Alliance Partners*?

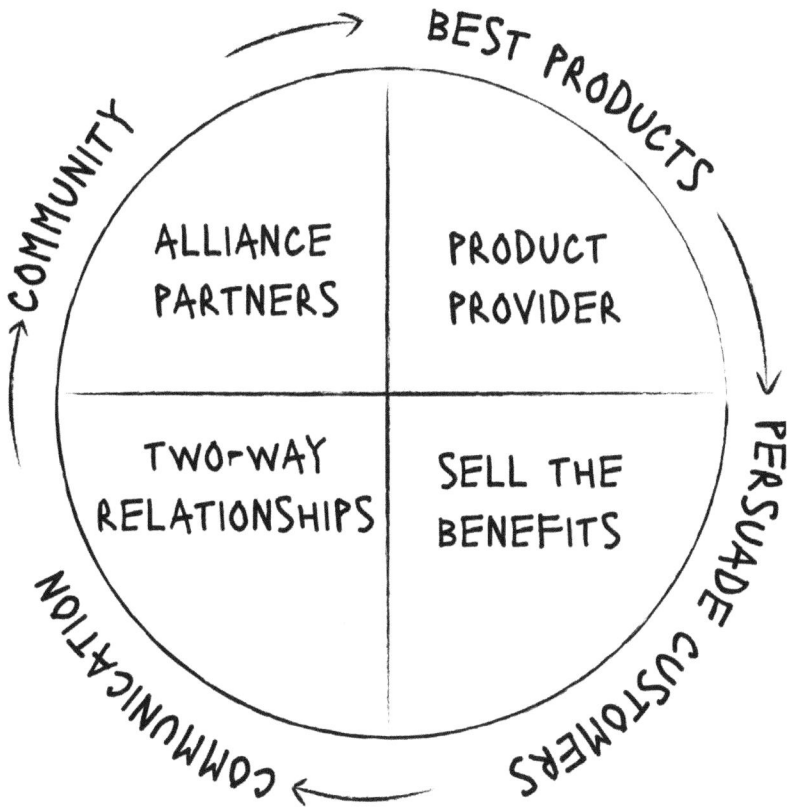

BEST PRODUCTS

COMMUNITY

PERSUADE CUSTOMERS

COMMUNICATION

| ALLIANCE PARTNERS | PRODUCT PROVIDER |
| TWO-WAY RELATIONSHIPS | SELL THE BENEFITS |

"A good leader doesn't get stuck behind a desk."

Richard Branson

ICE CREAM VANS ON THE BEACH

Reduce Customer Search Costs

Unless you are like Apple or Coca Cola, it's likely 99% of people in the world have never heard of your business. They have never met someone from your company and are unaware of you. Even if you have paid thousands for internet advertising, a general web search for your product classification is still unlikely to connect you with a vast number of potential buyers. However, if you can leverage your small reputation with a competitor's reputation, things might look a little different.

Overlooked stakeholders are competitors. Overlooked, because of the untapped value that exists in sharing places, spaces, resources and even customers with competitors. When shopping, I have often been referred on to a business by its competitor. This happened when a customer-focused employee knew their store was out of stock or that a competitor was offering something that better suited my needs. My sense of loyalty to the business referring was strengthened. The lifetime value of loyal repeat customers far exceeds the value of a few lost sales.

Since 2010, both Apple and Amazon have shared similar market spaces, resources and customers. Amazon's Kindle Reader was eclipsed by the Apple iPad release in 2009 and by 2010, Apple released new software for Kindle Books on the iPad. Even though this created competition for Amazon's Kindle E-Reader sales, this new connection between the competitors dramatically increased sales for both. As a result, Apple sold more iPads and Kindle sold more e-books; and in the long run,

Amazon sold more of its Kindle E-Readers than it would have done without Apple.

Imagine a long beach on a hot day, covered with thousands of people. An ice cream van arrives. Where should it park? When I ask my conference audiences, they all agree that the middle of the beach will be the best place to start trading. Now imagine a second ice cream van arrives. Where should it park? Around 50% of my audience believe the best spot is at one end of the beach. The others think it is next to the first van – which is the right answer. Unless the first van had been selling rancid ice cream, it is rational to set up right alongside it. The second van benefits from the growing reputation of the first van and the first van benefits from the added social proof of having a second van adjacent. In time, previously unaware beachgoers will know that one can purchase ice cream from the middle of the beach. Customer search costs are reduced. Customer confidence increases with each new van.

With two vans, 1 + 1 = 3. Both vans enjoy extra sales. Now imagine a third van arriving. Still, 30% of my audience feel the third van should head for one end of the beach. The best location for the third van and subsequent vans is adjacent to the others[16]. Now, 1+1+1=5 and 1+1+1+1=7, etc. This is why competing telco outlets in malls have adjacent shop fronts, why other furniture retailers locate right next to IKEA stores, why there are 41 theatres between 7th and 8th Avenues on Broadway and why Chinese restaurants in a Chinatown precinct will enjoy a reputation that allows them to make more sales than a stand-alone Chinese restaurant – even one in a busy part of town.

If the quality of ice cream in adjacent vans falls off or if shows on Broadway lose their edge, it may be time to move away. Being one of the growing new shows in nearby Greenwich Village might help new players create a successful Off-Broadway scene. Six factors: brand reputation, product quality, speed of service, ongoing support, price and customer searching costs are all critical for success. By keeping one's competitors close without colluding on price, which is illegal, and modifying the menu a little, maybe we can improve all six.

A business can succeed in reducing customer search costs and increasing sales by staying connected to their competitors' activities and moves. Many winning businesses seek to be both similar to and different from their competitors. Winning businesses stay connected with customers, employees, and business partners at the exploration, development, and execution stages of strategy. The most successful businesses also check the competitive landscape at each stage, by having a healthy competitor orientation.

ACTIVITY 3.2
COMPETITOR ORIENTATION

1. On the blank pages opposite, create a list of all your **Competitors**. Give each player and yourself a score out of ten, for each of the six aspects of brand reputation, product quality, speed of service, ongoing support, price and customer search costs. What can you learn from your competitors? What new standards of performance should you adopt?

2. For each competitor, come up with three creative ways to reduce customer search costs, increase customer confidence and **grow the size of the pie for all players**. Apple and Amazon grew the overall size of the pie for e-book sales while carving off big slices for themselves. Can you work alongside a competitor legally and increase the size of the pie for both of you? If so, write down which slice of the pie you want. While still leaving a beautiful piece for your complementary competitor, decide how big you'd like your slice to be? How will you achieve this?

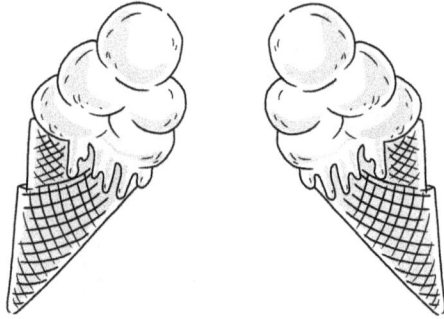

US   THEM

1 _____

2 _____

3 _____

4 _____

5 _____

6 _____

*"You have competition every day because you set such high standards
for yourself that you have to go out every day and live up to that."*

Michael Jordon

THE ROAD LESS TRAVELLED

Take the High Road

The road less travelled may be less travelled for a reason. Not all roads are profitable or ethical. Ten years ago, Chris, a friend who worked as a consultant, shared with me that his daily rate had recently tripled. Chris had offered his services to a weapons manufacturer, who was selling arms to groups across his region of the world.

I remember wrestling with Chris's reasoning and the idea of selling weapons. Chris and I attended fortnight-long retreats, where we practiced Zen inquiry. Chris was smart, but perhaps less enlightened. His skills were being used to create more dangerous weapons at faster rates. At the time, I had been working on a Strategic Plan with a City Council, for one-fifth of Chris's new rate. In the end, it came down to a difference in values and ethics. I cared about where those weapons ended up. Chris cared more about the money he earned.

Leaders who have earned our trust weigh up options carefully and are prepared to say, "There is no way that is happening on my watch." Over time, companies like 3M, Accenture and Xerox have enjoyed 'hard to copy' strategic advantages, due to reputations of highly ethical conduct. While numerous other firms through poor conduct are weakened in the eyes of customers, e.g. Nestle – for their role in harming children through the unethical promotion of infant formula, Monsanto – for their role in poisoning millions of people for decades, BHP – for polluting the Ok Tedi and Fly Rivers in New Guinea, which destroyed downstream villages and ecosystems and Shell – for their socially unconscionable drilling in the Netherlands, their human rights abuses in Nigeria and their highly questionable anti-climate financial lobbying of governments.

There are three questions one must ask. One, is this next step legal? For example, are we in breach of another's Intellectual Property (IP) and hence, do we have the freedom to continue operating? Two, does this next step maximize the profits from investments made? And three, is this next step ethical? If the answer to any of the three questions is 'no', it is not the road to take. If the answer is 'yes' to all three, then that road is worth considering. When planning strategy, best practice means keeping these ethical principles[17] in mind.

1. **Fiduciary** – act in the best interest of the company and investors
2. **Property** – respect property and the rights of those who own it
3. **Reliability** – keep promises, agreements and commitments
4. **Transparency** – conduct business truthfully and openly
5. **Dignity** – respect the dignity of others
6. **Fairness** – deal fairly with all parties
7. **Citizenship** – act as responsible members of the community
8. **Responsiveness** – respond to legitimate concerns of others

A legitimate concern for leaders can occur when a legally sound and seemingly ethical imperative to act erodes profitability. The moral leader chooses consciously to erode profitability for ethical conduct. When faced with this situation, the noble leader must go ahead with the ethical action and disclose the effect on profits to shareholders and relevant stakeholders. For a loyal employee who is incentivised to maximise profits and keep their job, knowing the right thing to do is often tricky. Ethics are often situational and are shaped by individual preferences, values, risk profiles and needs.

Behaviour consistent with a firm's Mission Statement and Stated Values can sometimes place a firm at a short-term competitive disadvantage. If this occurs, the best way forward is to work within the rules and find a creative way to make the competition less relevant, by promoting ethical behaviour as a long-term competitive advantage. A firm that fails ethically once, should not be defined by their mistake. However, if a culture of managers looks the other way when wrongdoing continues, regulation and harsh penalties from regulators are needed.

Stakeholders worth considering are regulators, governments, policy advisors and political influencers. The 'rules of the game' in which a business plays are changed occasionally by these groups. These same rules of the game can also be shaped by you as a proactive player, if you connect regularly with these stakeholder groups, during your strategy formulation and implementation process. The rules of the game keep changing. Where possible and ethical to do so, dialogue with regulators, government policymakers and lobbyists can help to highlight the real issues arising in your marketplace. Maybe you can help shape the rules for the better. Knowing the new rules of the game at the exploration, development and execution stages of strategy will help you win and do the right thing.

ACTIVITY 3.3
RULES OF THE GAME

1. On the blank pages opposite, make a list of the **Regulators**, including political influencers, government agencies, legal and industry bodies, who are involved in policy creation, regulation, and compliance.

2. Write down what you can do ethically, to ensure the voice of your business and your industry is considered, as regulators are shaping new rules. Also, note any potential **breach of IP issues** that exist in operating your business.

3. What **Ethical Principles** are often breached in your industry? Is there dishonest marketing by competitors, who make spurious or misleading product claims? What can you do to ensure ethical behaviour from members of your firm or organisation, as well as ecosystem partners in your extended business enterprise? Being proactive with ethical behaviour will significantly reduce risks to your brand and reputation.

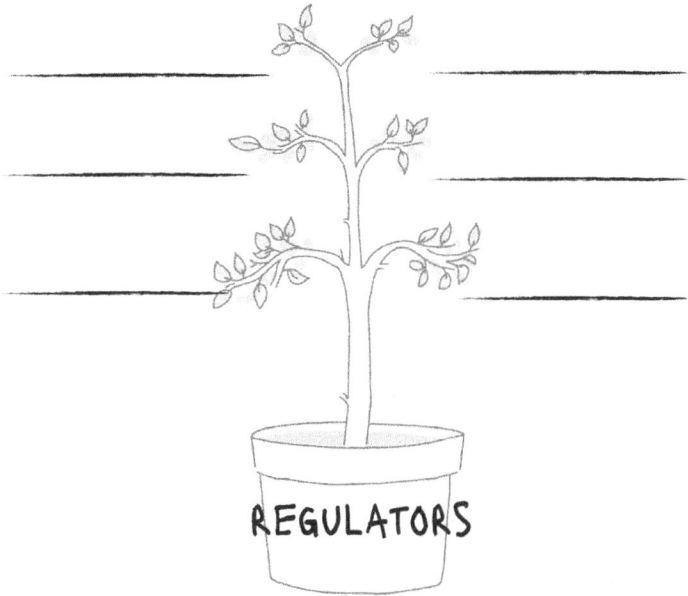

REGULATORS

GOOD   BAD   UGLY

"Without ethics, man has no future. This is to say, mankind without them cannot be itself. Ethics determine choices and actions and suggest difficult priorities."

John Berger

PLAN FUTURE VALUE

VALUE CHAINS

Integration Options

Industry structures shift over time. Rules of the game change. Buyers and suppliers may lose or gain power. Digital innovation can allow new players to enter and cause established players to leave; especially where substitution is occurring. For example, Encyclopedia Britannica's Claim to Fame was in large hardcover up-to-date reference book sets. Encyclopedia Britannica was forced out after CD-ROM and Wikipedia arrived. The profitability of an industry contributes to the profitability of the companies within it. However, the activities that a company performs within its industry and its position relative to other players also affects profits.

To maximize profits, companies must routinely plan with an up-to-date understanding of their industry and adjust their position relative to other players. This brings us to the fourth step in the six-step Strategic Mindset Process, which is to plan future value chains, creations and combinations.

Michael Porter brilliantly identified the Industry Value Chain as a set of activities that a firm operating in a specific industry performs to deliver a valuable product or service to the market[18]. The Industry Value Chain includes the sequence of activities needed to design, source, produce, sell, deliver and support customers. Firms position themselves at different points in an Industry Value Chain. For example, in the building construction industry, architects provide design services.

Building suppliers manufacture aluminum window frames and source materials upstream from smelters, which source bauxite upstream from mining firms. Property developers deliver the finished building. Further downstream in the Value Chain, realtors sell and rent finished apartments and offices. Insurance firms support property owners by helping to cover potential losses from future building damage.

The potential for value creation in each part of the Value Chain is different. Removing bauxite from the ground is not as valuable as converting it to aluminum window frames. The value created by the design is not as valuable as the work done to construct the building. The value captured can be different too. The realtor may do little for their commission. Likewise, the insurance firm may collect a lifetime of annual premiums for thousands of building apartments, while rarely having to pay a claim.

Over time, companies move positions along the industry Value Chain in ways that leverage their capabilities to create new value and claim more significant profits. In terms of backward Value Chain integration, Apple has made moderately successful moves upstream into microchip manufacturing; seizing value from Motorola, who had enjoyed Apple as a customer. Google moved backward into operating systems and Amazon into publishing. These players, despite some success, have learnt that backwards or upstream moves are often more susceptible to exploitation by other players than downstream moves.

In forward Value Chain integration, Apple has made highly successful downstream moves into Retail Stores. Google into Home Innovation and Amazon into Banking. Downstream moves give players who forward integrate greater influence over the end user or customer. Vertical

Integration is the term used for movements forward and downstream along the Value Chain, as well as movements backwards and upstream.

Horizontal Integration is mastering an activity in one part of the Value Chain and turning it into a new product or service. Apple moved horizontally by re-selling memory chips from traded iPads and iPhones, where Apple earned more than all the remaining players in the memory industry! Google Maps, Amazon Cloud, and Amazon Global Logistics are other examples of horizontal integration. In summary, performing different activities from other players can create a source of competitive advantage – as does performing activities differently. Good strategy includes unique tailoring of the value chain. Unique activity choices on the supply side are matched up with corresponding and coherent activity choices on the demand side to create unique competitive advantages. The standardized activities chosen by a firm, help to create the Capability Platform by which their strategy succeeds or fails. Proper alignment between the Capability Platform, sources of advantage and the strategy are crucial for success.

ACTIVITY 4.1
FUTURE VALUE CHAIN

1. On the blank pages opposite, map out your **Industry Value Chain** with labels, boxes, and connecting arrows. Make a list of players, including your firm, that exist at each step of the Value Chain. Do any players perform the same activities? Do they perform them

differently? Why? What is their Claim to Fame? How is it different from your Claim to Fame?

2. Decide where the most value is created and captured in the Industry Value Chain. Is it upstream or downstream from you? Are there new value-creating activities in either direction, where you would have a relative cost advantage, price advantage, or up-scalable potential over existing players? If you are not sure, find out! What new capabilities and activities could you add to your **Capability Platform** that would make your offering incredibly popular, rare and valuable? Which activities could be outsourced or eliminated, so you can focus better in other areas?

3. Sketch out the next iteration of your firm's Value Chain, with labels, boxes and connecting arrows. Your firm's Value Chain will be a subset or extension of the Industry Value Chain. Sketch where you would like to move to and away from. Show which activities could change. Show where new players are needed. Write down your new or updated Claim to Fame, if a change of emphasis is now needed.

4. Consider horizontal integration. If you could significantly and masterfully increase the market reach of one of your activities without changing its position in the Value Chain, write down the options available to you.

5. Finally, how well does your Capability Platform align with your adjusted Value Chain and any new or updated Claim to Fame? Review who you identified as your customers. Be clear on exactly

where you are positioning yourself with your adjusted Value Chain. How will you reach your customers from here? Is there a threat that a customer could seize value from you by undertaking the activities you perform? Write down what might be needed to **align your Capability Platform with your new Value Chain**.

PROFIT MARGIN _____

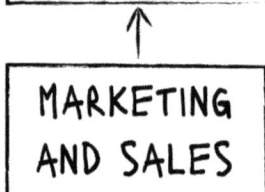

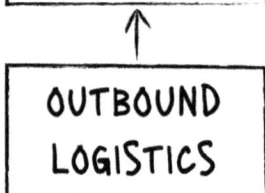

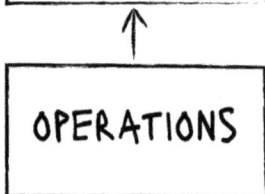

↑

| SERVICE | _____ |

↑

| MARKETING AND SALES | _____ |

↑

| OUTBOUND LOGISTICS | _____ |

↑

| OPERATIONS | _____ |

↑

| INBOUND LOGISTICS | _____ |

"Over the last decade, Ford has actually earned
more money making loans than making cars."

Adam Brandenburger

CREATE UNIQUE VALUE

Combine Known Things

When PepsiCo combined its popular cola drink with weight consciousness and created Diet Pepsi, it combined two known things. It wasn't the first to do so; in 1958, Diet Rite and TAB were the first movers. However, PepsiCo was a fast follower and captured an increased share of the soft drink market before Diet Coke entered. When Apple integrated the MP3 player with its iTunes Music Store and created the iPod, it combined two known things in a unique, rare and valuable way. This formula worked so well that the iPod eventually became an iTouch; which was then combined with a camera, a phone, a GPS, a tablet, and a wristwatch to create iPhones, iPads, and Apple Watches.

Combining two known things in unique, rare and valuable ways is at the heart of the creative process. In business, innovative teams routinely take a known thing they already have, say a product or service, and combine it with another known thing, to create a product or service extension. Amazon started as a struggling online bookstore. It eventually combined its online store with mainstream retail products and Amazon is now the world's biggest retailer. Amazon challenged the assumption that most people would only buy products they could see and touch. While in parallel, PayPal challenged the convention that people would only permit the transfer of money via their banks, rather than from person to person.

In his book *Strategy by Design*, James Carlopio challenges various conventional approaches to strategy, for 'design innovation' as a necessary complement to rational logic and analysis. James asserts that the creation of new ideas can come about by 'applying something that works in one area to another area, reversing direction whenever a direction is implied, and denying things that are taken for granted.'[19]

On summertime hunting trips, beneath the breath-taking snow-capped Swiss Alps in the 1940s, George de Mestral was inspired by the tiny hooks of cockleburs that were stuck on his pants and in his dog's fur. By applying something that worked in one area to another area, he invented Velcro – a rare and unique innovation that has in part, replaced taken-for-granted fastening methods like buttons, press studs, shoelaces, and the often-problematic zipper.

Another way to innovate is to limit what is permitted. Through the self-imposition of constraints, it becomes possible to transform weaknesses into strengths. Audi Racing's three successive 24-hour La Mans wins in the early 2000s resulted from their acceptance of a weakness. They accepted that they might never create the most powerful engine or the fastest car[20]. They constrained their new engine design process and reversed their thinking to combine racing cars with diesel engines – which drove slower but required fewer fuel stops than faster petrol engines. Less fuel stops over 24 hours allowed them to win! In 2017, Audi placed an ambitious new constraint on themselves, which was to build a winning all-electric car[21].

Millions of people sold their 'less often used' second family car once Uber combined a user-friendly ride service with the smartphone. The marriage between Global Positioning System phone software and private car owners wanting to earn extra dollars was a unique and valuable idea that bridged two previously unconnected ideas.

ACTIVITY 4.2
INNOVATIVE IDEAS

1. On the blank pages opposite jot down a list of the **Innovative Ideas** that make up your product, service or business model. Try combining what you do with seemingly unrelated things, perhaps inspired by nature, to come up with creative and outrageous ideas and options for product, service or business model extensions. Write down three new ideas which apply something that works in one area to another area. Try finding new value and untapped synergies in the intersection of two opposites. Pair mutually exclusive ideas in a totally new context. Try reversing direction whenever a direction is implied. What other ideas can you jot down?

2. List some widely held **Assumptions** about your industry, consumer behavior, and society in general. For example, banks are safe places to deposit savings, married people are happy, governments will care for the elderly, prescription drugs make life better, prisons reform criminals, fresh food markets are safer than supermarkets, or public and household Wi-Fi zones are harmless. Note that upon reflection, some of our assumptions may indeed be irrational, despite being

commonplace and taken for granted by most people. Can you push the boundaries of these assumptions, so they break, bend or blend into new forms? What new value could you add if these assumptions were successfully challenged and defeated through innovative thinking?

3. Write down areas where you may always have a competitive weakness. As an exercise, accept that you will never be the biggest, fastest, prettiest or most affordable. What **Constraint** could you use on yourself to narrow your firm's innovation focus to create something new, in a rare and uniquely valuable way? Jot down the innovative ideas that flow from placing this constraint on your future design activities.

4. Reflect on your list of innovative ideas. Keep imagining. Schedule four one-hour meetings to share ideas with four other people from unrelated industries. Take along plenty of paper and some 2B or 4B pencils and leave all judgements and preconceptions at the door. Don't be lazy. Don't fear failure. Remember it is always easier to be a critic than a creator! **Sharing and Brainstorming** with a diverse range of people, who are removed from your business, can enhance the value of the future you are creating. Finally, when you brainstorm, make sure you spend most of your time brainstorming for better questions. Better questions lead to better ideas.

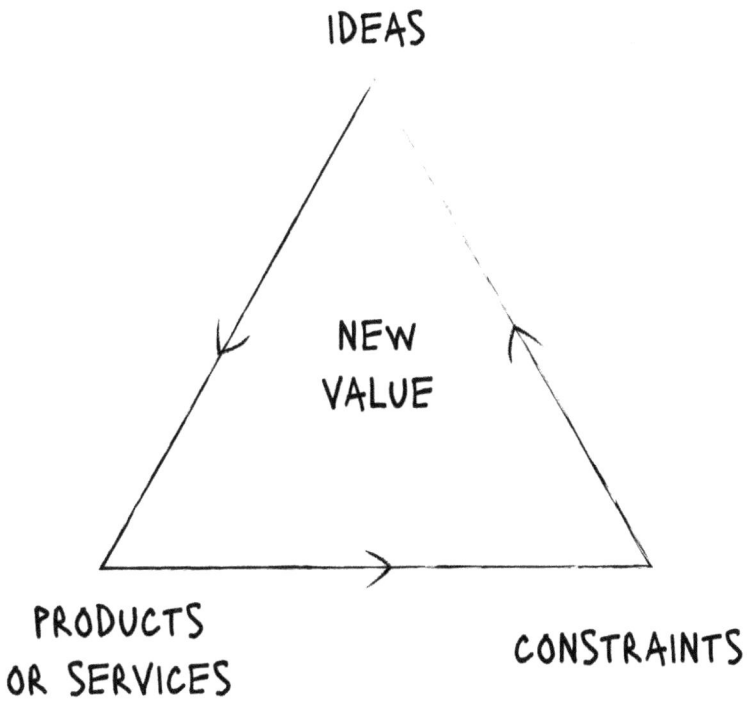

"I think being on a constraint with money makes you much more creative."

Anne Wojcicki

VALUE COMBINATIONS

Shaping the Future

Doing a quick search with the keywords, "evolution of surfboard shape" will display images of surfboards, that comprise curves. Notice that over time the shape, size and combinations of curves have changed. Old boards, like the one my grandfather owned in the 1920s, were long flat timber planks with a single curve on the nose. In the 1920s, businesses were similar to surfboards. There were very few curves or combinations. Ford Motor Company's Model T Automobile came in one variety, which was black.

The variety and value of surfboards, automobiles and businesses have increased. By raising the standard of what we offer and creating new features, we can provide customer value never seen before. By eliminating some features and reducing others, new combinations become possible.

When formulating new combinations, we can eliminate, reduce, raise and create various factors. The size of surfboards has been reduced. Wood was eliminated for fiberglass and styrene foam. The size of car wheels has been reduced and early solid rubber tires were eliminated and replaced with pneumatic tires. In business, factors are also reduced and eliminated. The recent move away from the traditional law firm to the New Law business model has included reductions in lawyer stress and in-house expertise. New Law businesses are ordering priorities in a new way. They have eliminated the need for palatial offices, large teams and partner profit sharing. New Law has found new ways to put customer considerations ahead of firm considerations.

Auto manufacturers and surfboard-making businesses have also raised the standard offered and created value never seen before. New Law has raised standards by providing levels of service affordability, such as 'no win, no fee' and standardized contracts. They have created 24/7 advice via virtual meetings, smart contracts and flexible family-friendly work hours for staff. Over the last century, Ford and its competitors have raised the standard of tires and car colors. More combinations are available in the modern car than ever before.

The modern surfboard has raised maneuverability and speed via rocker curves, rail curves, tail curves, and curved fins. In Western Australia and South Africa, Rusty Surfboards have been painting shark repelling zig-zag zebra curves on the underside of surfboards to help save the lives of surfers. No ocean stays shark-free forever. Businesses must formulate increasingly valuable combinations to survive and thrive.

A business may one day need to rationalize or exit. When product or service offerings are needed less and less, it's hard to let go. When backward integration is not wise, forward integration impossible and horizontal integration is not aligned with a firm's Capability Platform, then rationalizing the scope of the business may be prudent. Exiting may also be prudent. Liquidation of any remaining assets and refunding shareholders or investors is an often overlooked and at times wise strategic move. 'Throwing good money after bad' can perpetuate an already vicious death spiral. Kim and Mauborgne's Four Actions Framework[22] in the activity below offers four questions that help businesses plan for the future, formulate valuable new combinations, rationalize, or exit.

ACTIVITY 4.3
FOUR ACTIONS FRAMEWORK

1. On the blank pages opposite, jot down your ideas for Reducing what you offer, perhaps below the current standard expected by your industry or marketplace, e.g., the market expected a taxi to be mid-sized with a decent boot for suitcases. Uber offered customers the choice of smaller cars to capture new value for both parties. In response, some traditional taxi companies rationalized and exited. Others stayed put to reduce, eliminate, raise and create factors, until they successfully reshaped their existing value combinations in sensible ways

2. List your ideas for Eliminating something you offer, which you or others have taken for granted until now, e.g., inflight meals, supermarket shopping, bank branches, human-centric legal advice and retail stores. Regular elimination of underperforming and less valuable activities allows for the reallocation of scarce resources to more promising and proven activities and factors that need to be raised or created.

3. Write out your ideas for Raising the standard of something you offer, well above the current standard expected by your industry or marketplace, e.g., 24/7 support, real-time device apps or free shipping. Good strategy is about making trade-offs and the reallocation of resources that raise standards in how you operate and what you offer. If you have to choose between resource allocation for technological advancement or resource allocation for global distribution, choosing the former over the latter will likely be prudent.

4. Include some ideas for Creating something radical never offered before, e.g., Digital wallets, smart pillboxes, vibrating sleep bracelets, deep-water submersibles, very high-speed trains, and passenger drones. The sky is the limit. How will you push the boundaries in your marketplace and shape the future with new yet familiar, unique, rare, scalable and valuable products or services?

5. Reflect on your answers. Schedule four one-hour meetings to share ideas with four other people from somewhat related industries. Take along plenty of paper and some colored or 2B or 4B pencils. **Sharing and Brainstorming** with people from nearby industries can offer new perspectives on what might constitute new, radical and relevant value combinations.

6. As you start choosing a new value-driven strategy, involve your people with its development. This step offers significant benefits when it comes time to implement the strategy.

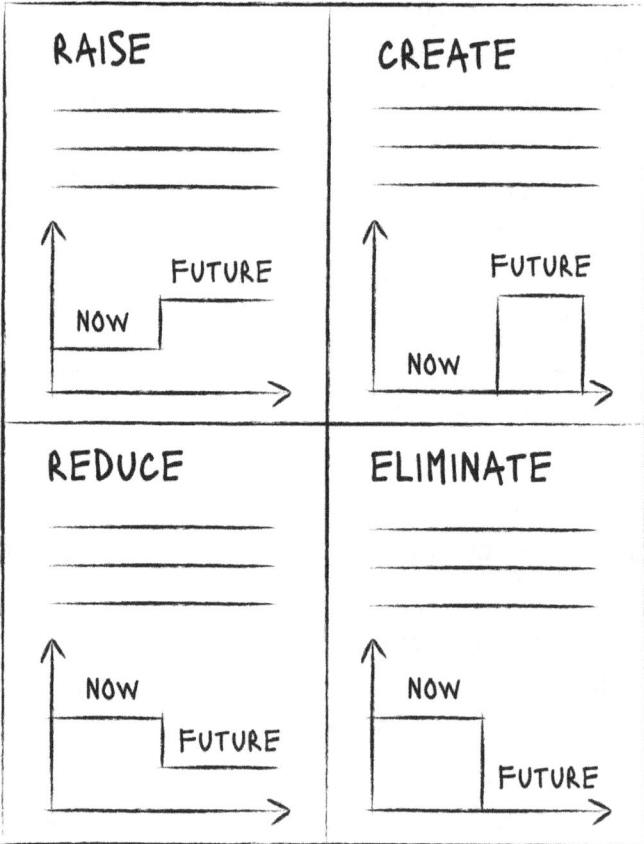

"Every company wants one, yet few companies have one: a compelling strategy."

W. Chan Kim, Renée Mauborgne

FOCUS ON A CHOSEN TARGET

ON TARGET

Shoot for the Moon

Confucius once said, "The man who chases two rabbits, catches neither." We often keep both rabbits in our sights. Chase one rabbit. Choosing one increases our chance of success. This brings us to the fifth step in the six-step Strategic Mindset Process, which is to focus on a chosen target. Steve Jobs made small computers rather than the world's biggest computer. Audi Racing won when they made the most efficient diesel racing car rather than the fastest. Be on target. If you miss, refocus and keep going. Overnight successes are rare. Persist. Slow progress is still progress. If progress stops, sense, see, connect, plan and then choose a new target.

When choosing a target, be bold. Goethe is credited with the statement, "Whatever you can do or dream you can, begin it; Boldness has genius, power, and magic in it."[23] In 1962, President J. F. Kennedy said, "We choose to go to the moon." Seven years later, Apollo 11 landed on the moon and then returned safely to Earth. The moon was a good target. Bold yet near enough to be reached. Targeting space travel to the moon resulted in many benefits. The list of over two-thousand spin-off products coming from NASA includes memory foam, freeze-dried food, space blankets, dust busters, LZR Racer swimsuits, artificial limbs, scratch-resistant lenses, aircraft anti-icing, water purification, and solar cells[24].

NASA was bold and achieved many great things by staying on target. When we choose a big hairy audacious goal (BHAG) [25], even if we don't reach it, we will likely be better off than when we started. We can still miss a target and create a great deal of value. Businesses with well-governed R&D behind them are worth more. 'Shoot for the moon. Even if you miss, you'll land among the stars[26]'. A man who seems to have shot for the stars and learnt a lot is Sir Richard Branson. Richard always had a target. Virgin Cola, Virgin Bridal, Virgin Clothing, Virgin Student, Virgin Express, Virgin Pulse, Virgin Digital, and Virgin Flowers bloomed overnight and then withered. But Virgin Airways, Virgin Money, Virgin Trains, Virgin Hotels, and other holiday-related ventures flourished. I suspect Branson chased a few too many rabbits, yet he focused long enough to choose clear targets.

Clear, bold, valuable targets have three well-defined elements. The first is a defined <u>objective</u>. The second is a defined **domain**. The third is a clearly defined *unfair advantage*. Branson was good at the first two elements while perhaps struggling with the third. One of the world's most successful businesses is IKEA. The IKEA business strategy's target includes the three aspects of <u>objective</u>, **domain**, and *unfair advantage*.

<u>We offer a wide range</u> *of well-designed, functional* <u>home furnishing products</u> *at prices so low* **that as many people as possible will be able to afford them**[27].

Unlike 'one-stop' megastores, IKEA did not choose to sell sound systems, computers, televisions, vacuum cleaners, phones or car accessories. IKEA chose to be a low-priced integrated home and office furniture 'category killer'. Apple chose to be a high-priced integrated personal and professional computing category specialist. Are you sitting on the fence? Have you been trying to be all things to all people? Are you low-cost or do you offer a premium-priced service? How will you sharpen the scope of your offering? Look for the best combinations of objective, **domain** and *unfair advantage* that offer you the most scalable options. Size is not everything, but as Velcro, Ray Kroc, Apple, IKEA, Amazon, NASA and Uber have shown us, being big can change the world and your profitability for the better. Does your business model scale easily? Could your firm become a bigger player in your own category?

ACTIVITY 5.1
MISSION STATEMENT

1. Review your Claim to Fame and your industry's Critical Success Factors while remembering your updated Value Chain, Value Creations and Value Combinations. Then on the blank pages opposite write down all the areas where you already have or can create an *unfair advantage* over other players.

2. Who could be your ideal customers, both now and in the future? What **domain** do you want to serve with your product or service?

3. Drill down, review your objective and choose a clearly defined, and scalable target.

4. Reflect on your chosen *unfair advantage*, **domain,** and objective. In consultation with your entire team and key stakeholders – like customers, suppliers and investors, write out a **Mission Statement** with three equal parts. One third that articulates your *unfair advantage*, one third that deals with **domain**, and one third that clarifies your primary objective.

5. Finally, can you fashion your mission statement into a **Mantra**? A Mantra is a three-or-four-word statement that crystalizes and embodies your mission even more succinctly. It acts to reinforce your clarity of purpose for all. Apple's mantra is "Think different"; Nike's is "Authentic athletic performance"; Disney's is "Fun family entertainment"; FedEx's is "Peace of Mind" and Australian Icon B&D Doors' is "Home Safe Home". On the blank pages opposite, see if you can create a Mantra that helps communicate your customer or employee focused strategic intent.

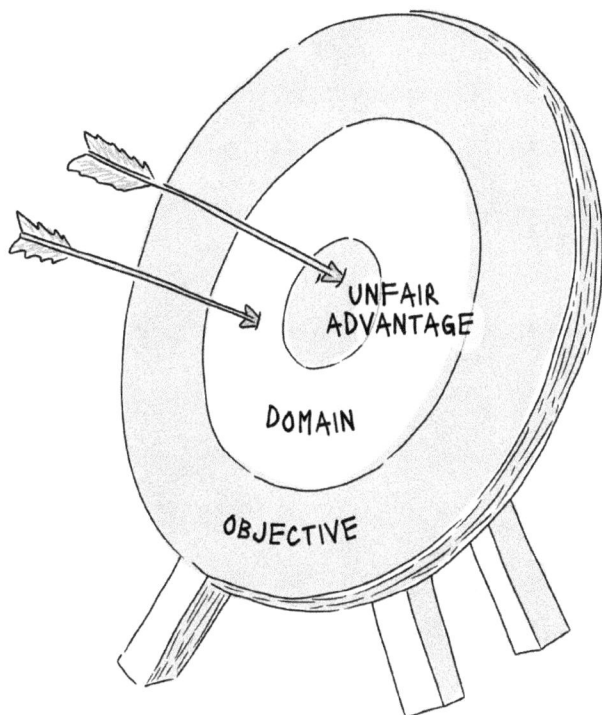

MISSION _____

_____

_____

_____

MANTRA _____

"Good strategy works by focusing energy and resources on one, or a very few, pivotal objectives whose accomplishment will lead to a cascade of favorable outcomes."

Richard Rumelt

CHOOSE

What not to do

In life and business, choosing is often tricky. Very few of us have cultivated the discipline of really choosing – it is hard work. We like to have it all. When choosing one thing over another, one person over another, or one activity over another, a decision is needed. The word decide comes from the Latin root, which means to 'cut off'. Strategy is about making good choices and eliminating bad ones. Yet options are not always clear. Many seemingly good decisions have a downside and many bad choices have some upside. Choosing where to play and how to win comes down to value. We must create value but capture it too. Letting go of average customers can free your people up to serve the customers you really want.

Apple iPhone pricing is a good example of ignoring the many and serving the few. By continually increasing the product quality and price of the iPhone, Apple attracts premium buyers from select outlets all over the world. The downside of this approach was that in 2020, the iPhone was still too expensive for the India phone market – a huge market that could double iPhone sales overnight if Apple lowered its features, prices and profit margins. Soon after, Apple hedged its bets a little and introduced a new moderately-priced iPhone SE.

Apple chose not to be a *Commodity Product*, where price is critical. Apple avoids being a *Convenience Product*, which relies predominantly on brand reputation and wide networks of distribution. Apple has chosen to be a *Premium Shopping Product* – something that requires an informed purchasing decision, where superior product quality, extra features and extended warranties will mostly outweigh a reliance on brand, price or a wide distribution of sales outlets. In the Business to Business marketplace, a choice between *Premium Shopping Products* and *Commodity Products* plays out, where brand and distribution networks are not usually relevant.

Winning businesses make trade-offs to protect both sales and profit margins. Firms that do not make trade-offs but offer all the same features as their rivals will eventually create a price war and a race to the bottom, where profitability will be close to zero. In markets with only two players, innovation stalls and players collude on price. In the 1980s, with only two airlines in Australia, I remember a domestic flight was closer to $500 than today's price of $150. In the 1990s with only two telephone companies in Australia, phone calls were expensive and monthly mobile phone bills were greater than today's annual bill. As more airlines and phone companies entered offering similar services, price wars ensued.

Being similar to others is like the Ice Cream Vans on the Beach metaphor, where adjacent businesses, via social proof and proximity, grow the overall market size together. However, if each Ice Cream Van offers the same three flavors of ice cream in the same cones and cups, they will create a price war and a race to the bottom. Locating ourselves adjacent to other players can be a wise move if we take proper notice of our rivals' value propositions and ensure we are unique and different. If a nearby van offers soft serve ice cream with berries, nuts and chocolate, we may choose to sell our soft serve machine and buy a big mobile freezer so we can sell multiple flavors of homemade ice cream. Making these sorts of trade-offs can be hard initially. Yet if we can get the right fit between different parts of the business, it can be worthwhile eventually.

Trade-offs mean accepting reality and thinking differently in ways that create new, unique and defendable value propositions. Ongoing research, working hard behind the scenes and inventing ice cream recipes which are innovative and hard to emulate can create a unique value proposition at a profitable price.

ACTIVITY 5.2
IDEAL CUSTOMER

1. On the blank pages opposite, write out ideas for what you could change in your product or service that over time, would be difficult for rivals to copy without negatively affecting their business? Will this change your value positioning so it moves you more or less into one of the three categories of being a **Commodity, Convenience, or Premium Shopping Product** or Service?

2. Adding features to a product or service often provides an advantage over competitors and an added benefit to customers. Consider reversing direction for a moment to help align your product or service with a new and more desirable category. Write down a

list of features, which if removed, might offer an unrealized gain or benefit?

3. If you could keep just 20% of your current customers and 20% of your current products or services, which combinations of each would you keep? How could you change your products or services to add even more value? How much more could you sell your product or service for? How many new customers could you reach?

4. In the context of the total addressable market, total revenue, total profit and where to play, reflect on your preferred choice moving forward. Describe your next generation of product or service offering, with its features, advantages, benefits, communities and alliance partners. Note how its value and pricing differ from your current, your past, and your competitors' offerings. Now write out a detailed description of your **Ideal Customer** and where they will purchase your product or service.

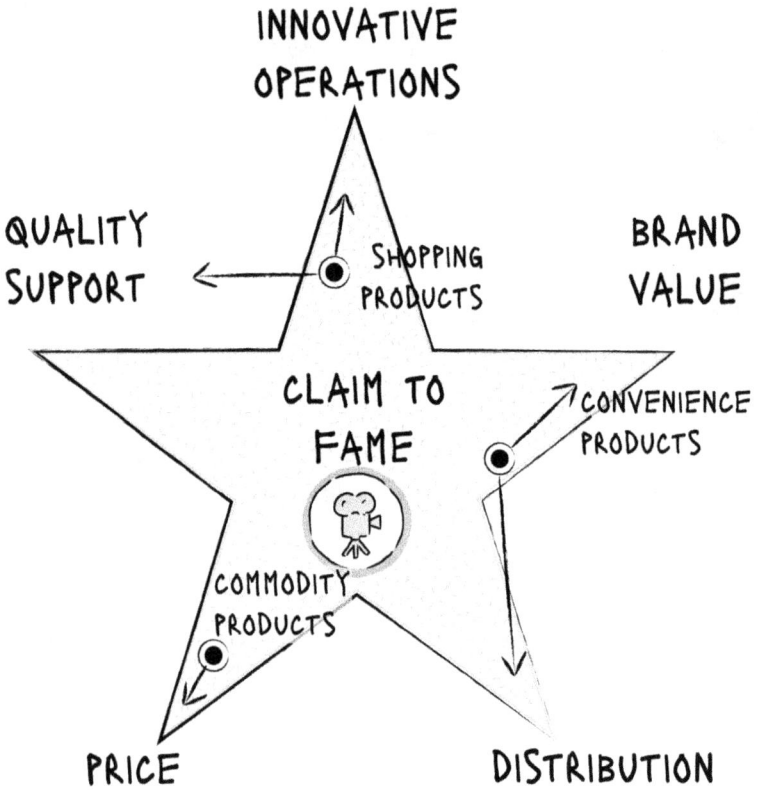

INNOVATIVE
OPERATIONS

QUALITY
SUPPORT

BRAND
VALUE

SHOPPING
PRODUCTS

CLAIM TO
FAME

CONVENIENCE
PRODUCTS

COMMODITY
PRODUCTS

PRICE

DISTRIBUTION

"There is no such thing as a commodity. It is simply
a product waiting to be differentiated."

Philip Kotler

FOCUS ON FACTS

Triangulate Skillfully

The English and French fought the Battles of Crecy in 1346 and Agincourt in 1415. The French soldiers were heavily armed 'Ironclads', drawn from the aristocracy of France. Most of the English forces were lightly plated Yeoman archers. At Crecy, the English army was 8,000 strong, 5,000 of which were archers. The French Ironclads were a 20,000 strong army on horseback – a seemingly unstoppable force[28].

Before the Battle of Crecy, King Edward III changed his focus and decided that his entire army would fight on their feet, without horses. His front line and two flanks were peppered with archers. In the ensuing battle, the French lost 16,000 men and the English 300. As the French army charged from a single position, bouncing on horseback, they could not focus clearly on any single chosen target. English archers had both feet planted firmly on the earth at one of three vantage points and were able to focus clearly on selected targets, one after the other.

The French also had archers, with mechanistic crossbows that took more time to load than the simple English longbows. In my conference talks, I sometimes take a crossbow and a longbow with me to demonstrate. I share the stories and tactics used to fight in the Battles of Crecy and Agincourt. I share that French arrogance was the deciding factor at the second battle in Agincourt. Instead of focusing and learning from their mistakes at Crecy, the French engineered metal visors for their helmets and added chainmail to their horses. At Agincourt, the single pointed charging and then retreating French lost 6,000 men out of 10,000, while the well-grounded English, again with archers on three flanks, lost 200 out of 2,000. Again, England's archers had their feet firmly planted and could focus clearly on their chosen target from three vantage points. Agincourt showed us that the prestigious French aristocracy clung to the technologies and tactics that served them in distant past glories[29], rather than focusing on the immediate facts at hand.

Our ability to see clearly, be grounded in the relevant facts, and focus skillfully, are critical to winning. Some leaders see the world clearly - their analysis, market research, and customer understanding are spot on. Other leaders have access to all the data they need, but due to fear, procrastination, arrogance, or short-term memory loss, they become distracted and lose direction.

To support a winning army or a winning business, leaders must avoid having people move in separate directions. Having everyone on the same page and focused requires coherence. Coherent decision-making needs the discipline of triangulating information. Triangulation requires leaders to verify the primary assumptions that underpin each decision from three independent vantage points. If the third step of the Strategic Mindset Process is being carried out, triangulation becomes easy. Ongoing connection with customers, stakeholders, regulators and even competitors, helps triangulation, coherent decision making, and our ability to focus.

ACTIVITY 5.3
STRATEGIC FOCUS

1. On the blank pages opposite write three headings: '**See Clearly**', '**Stay Grounded in the Facts**' and '**Focus Skilfully**'. Under each heading, jot down a list of activities you do regularly to support each.

2. How did you go? Discuss your lists with a colleague. Share and collect more ideas for helping to increase your own ability to focus effectively. Did other issues emerge, like motivation or confidence? Make a diary note to address these issues separately.

3. Write down all the major assumptions your firm has used to formulate its current approach. Which markets and which products have you assumed are the best to be in? What assumptions drive any current ideas about new markets or new and modified products? Come up with a **Triangulation Process** to retest each assumption. To triangulate information used for key decision making, aim to dialogue with three independent yet reliable sources, to test all your significant assumptions. Once you have triangulated all your assumptions, write down what you have learnt.

4. Reflect on your findings. If the triangulation feedback concurs and your revised assumptions are good, it may be time to get excited and choose likely winners from your current ideas. Because most people prefer new products that are somehow familiar, choosing an incremental approach to new product extensions and/or new market developments can be sensible. Too much **Product or**

Service Extension along with too much **Market Development** simultaneously is pure '**diversification**' and likely to be further away from where you started as a business and your Claim to Fame. Summarize your findings. **Pick what you must do to win** and write down what your future strategic focus should be. This exercise might yield a desirable new product or brand-new market that will require coherent changes to your guiding policies and business model. For example, this may be new goals, new activities, resources, channels to market or funding.

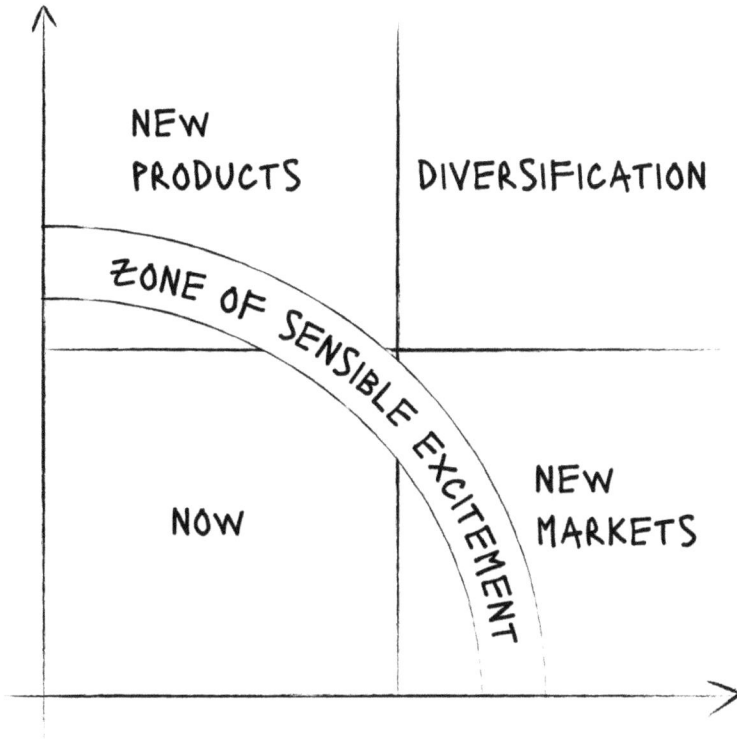

"If your goal is anything but profitability - if it's to be big, or to grow fast, or to become a technology leader - you'll hit problems."

Michael Porter

MOVE FASTER WITH INFLUENCE

NEED FOR SPEED

Be Ready to Jump

The sixth step in the Strategic Mindset Process is to move faster with influence. Suppose you carry out a Strategic Mindset Process every three years. This could be helpful in project planning and budgeting. Knowing ahead of time, which initiatives are to be funded and delivered each year, offers your people a clear direction, which they can count on. I have facilitated annual planning for some firms who lack the will and intelligence to jump when they needed to. I have spent days with them mapping their future. Yet, once we were done, they asked themselves the best way of fitting the new strategic direction into their predictable and predetermined budgets. Allowing 'the tail to wag the dog' can be a recipe for disaster!

Instead, suppose your success recipe includes carrying out the Strategic Mindset Process each quarter. The increased frequency of your process means that, as changes occur in the marketplace and new windows open, it becomes easy to jump in time to capitalize on them. By releasing the iPhone on 29 June 2007, Apple caught the then phone giant, Nokia, off-guard. By mid-June 2007, it was highly likely budgets and projects for the next twelve months would have been set and signed off by the Nokia Board. Over the following four years, Nokia struggled to make up ground. Meanwhile, Apple deliberately cannibalized product sales of its existing models by introducing newer and faster generations of smartphones, with increasingly higher prices.

The strategy process at Apple and many winning companies is neither annual nor quarterly. It is a dynamic and continuous pattern of innovative leadership thinking. Apple moves fast and brings its team along. Legendary General Electric CEO Jack Welch would rank his entire workforce regularly so he could give bonuses to the top 20%, fire or incite resignation from the bottom 10% and then have the funds to hire fresh talent[30]. Jack appreciated the need for speed by being proactive. Many companies frequently lose their star employees to higher-paying firms, while retaining a growing pool of underperforming staff and allowing their stagnant culture to kill any new strategy. Jack was different. He made sure the best people in the company did not jump ship and he weeded out poor performers regularly. It is worth noting that key performance metrics are representations of a company's strategy, but they are not the strategy.

No two companies are identical. Even similar firms operate in different markets and market segments. Each market has a speed to it and market speeds fluctuate over time. Some markets are slow cycle markets[31] and change may happen slowly, e.g. Banking, Insurance and Airlines. Some markets are standard cycle markets[32] and change may be steady, e.g. Automobiles, Medicine and Law. Other markets are fast cycle markets [33] and the pace of change may be spectacular, e.g. Manufacturing, Entertainment, and Logistics.

The rate of change in a market will determine the operational and strategic speeds needed to win in that market. The greater the potential for disruption that exists, the faster firms must think, adapt and adjust their operations. The impact of digital innovation in any market will be determined by that market's suitability to new and emerging technologies.

Fifty years ago, Law operated in a slow cycle market. Law has moved from a slow cycle market into a fast cycle market, due to the adoption of suitable new learning cognition technologies. AI systems have now learnt the rules and application of all known laws in a fraction of the time it used to take a person to do so, and then offer sound advice to clients at a reduced cost.

Slow cycle markets can be just as ripe for rapid innovation as fast cycle markets, providing the time is right and the capital investment to do so is not too high. Optimistic and option rich firms rarely fail from moving too fast. Millions of misguided and pessimistic firms we can no longer remember died from moving too slowly. They are also not around to share with us the importance of speed.

ACTIVITY 6.1
CHANGE OF PACE

1. On the blank pages opposite, write down a list of the markets you operate in. Decide if they are **Slow, Standard, or Fast Cycle Markets**. How ripe are they for change? Over time slow markets can speed up and fast markets may slow down. Noting our market's current velocity as well as the amount of creative potential and innovative fuel currently residing in our chosen industry will provide a more complete picture.

2. Jot down both current and **Future Technologies** that are affecting the way you will do business in the future. Are these technologies moving your way soon, for example, advanced robotics, speech cognition, passenger drones, and self-driving transporters?

3. Do you consider these future scenarios as threats, opportunities or options? Are you ready to jump? Agree with others **how frequently you will engage in the six-step Strategic Mindset Process.**

4. Reflect on your firm's understanding of time. Write down some key milestones in your business. Are there plans that you expect will take three years to realize? Now, underline all three-year milestones that could be reached in six months, with **real focus and faster execution.** Write down a distant and valuable milestone you could deliver in the next six months.

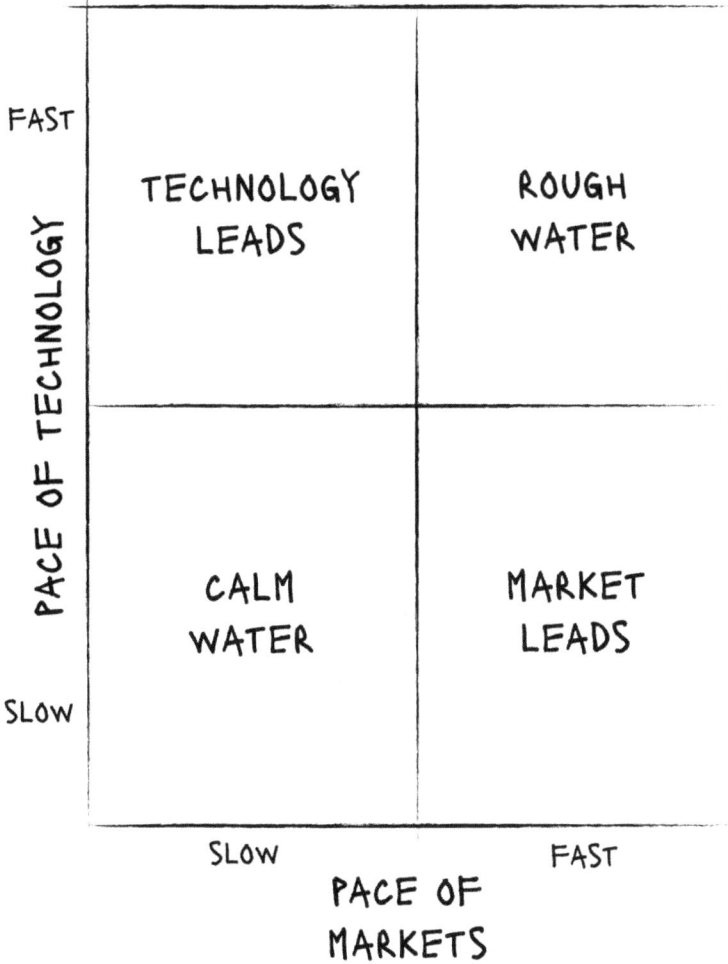

FAST

PACE OF TECHNOLOGY

| TECHNOLOGY LEADS | ROUGH WATER |
| CALM WATER | MARKET LEADS |

SLOW

SLOW — FAST

PACE OF MARKETS

"I've always found that the speed of the leader is the speed of the team."

Lee Iacocca

MOVE

Avoid Disaster and Win

Three impediments to movement are inertia, entropy, and bias. Bias is mostly unconscious. Our brains filter out information that contradicts existing mental maps. We make links between discrete pieces of information to create meaning. Because we can only remember so much, our brains take short cuts. This means at times we may shoot from the hip quickly without thinking. Many of us follow passing trends with limited knowledge, which can lead to disastrous results.

If the first five steps of the Strategic Mindset Process are followed, there is a good chance that, when it is time to move or shoot, it can be done with high awareness and great results. We may be the ones setting a valuable trend instead of following it. Sensing and seeing, connecting with customers, stakeholders and regulators, creating value and choosing a target, can make significant differences to how and when we move.

Your firm's next strategic move could be to head west and be the first to stake out new uncontested market spaces; stay put to grow bigger through slow continuous improvement; exit declining and less profitable product-markets; shake up the market by revitalizing an old trail that captures latent demand; consolidate and then deliberately wait for the next big thing; partner with others to fight back and shape the new rules of the game; create never before seen customer value with a compelling vision and scalable product or service; and then decide how the business will compete horizontally or vertically within the future Industry Value Chain and the new industries of the future.

Following the Strategic Mindset Process helps combat entropy and inertia. The Law of Entropy states that disorder increases in isolated systems. We avoid having isolated systems, by routinely sensing and seeing our external environment, embracing diversity, and sharing ideas openly with others. The Law of Inertia states that a body moving in a particular direction keeps moving in the same direction unless acted on by a force. Inertia is present when I hear a leader say, "This is the way we have always done it!" Even customers can suffer from inertia when their perceived switching costs[34] are no longer real. The first time the Strategic Mindset Process is followed, there may be a realization that one has been 'asleep in the wagon' and we have 'missed the turnoff to the future.[35]' Just as often, preoccupied managers can see the need for their company to jump and take the turnoff to the future, but due to inertia, they find it impossible. A future product or service idea may never take off due to a lack of procurement readiness or by having competing priorities and targets. External factors like regulatory frameworks, media backlashes, and market readiness may cause future initiatives to backfire and thwart any plans about scaling them up. Consequently, 'few managers devote much time to thinking about the future, and almost no time in developing initiatives to adapt to it.[36]'

The Strategic Mindset Process forces us to ask better questions, think differently, chart new horizons and jump quickly. Learning to jump, especially for large organizations, can be challenging. Windows of opportunity can open and close quickly. The smart handheld devices era was a wild ride. This new frontier opened quickly, crushing large players like Intel, Kodak, Motorola, Nokia, Blackberry, Sony, Blockbuster, TomTom, Garmin and the taxi industry, to name but a few. Fast movers and followers like Apple, Samsung and Huawei, won the early race for market share. For winning players, the new is never seen as a threat, only an opportunity to jump in.

Not jumping in is a valid move if it is done consciously. In the late 1990s, when asked about his next steps, Steve Jobs, who was looking for something he could scale, replied that he was waiting for the next big thing[37]. Successful companies are aware of windows of opportunity and make sure they are quick to jump through them and win. They may or may not be the first mover. They may be a fast second or third mover. However, they are one of the first few to get it right. Having all our ducks lined up helps. How ready are you? All the right pieces must align harmoniously. Running a business can be like a western film. In a shoot-out, the first to fire only wins if they are ready and their aim and alignment are true.

ACTIVITY 6.2
GET GOING

1. On the blank pages opposite, write down four words: Ready, Aim, Align, and Fire. Some firms fire first before they have a clear target. Others are not ready and can't deliver. Other firms die because they take too long to aim or don't align the right pieces. Rate out

of ten, your ability to be ready, aim well, align the right pieces, and to fire quickly.

2. What is your firm most proficient at? **Readying, Aiming, Aligning, or Firing**?

3. Where is your firm weakest? How can you win the next shoot-out? You must have a clear direction that your people trust. To win, you must think ahead of time, but also move fast. Unless of course your well-considered plan is to move slowly, because of a big recession, where tightening your belt for a time makes sense. You may also want to move slowly, if your strategy is to consolidate and then deliberately wait for the next big thing.

4. Reflect on inertia, entropy and bias. To evolve, a business must get better. We can't get any better until we get going. Put this book down and don't come back to it until you have successfully implemented an idea, action or strategy from it. **Off you go...**

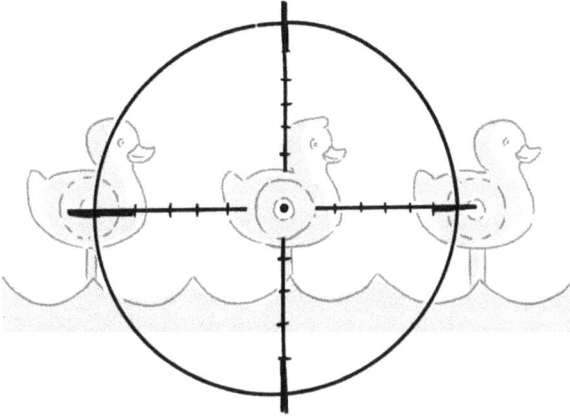

1. READYING _____

2. AIMING _____

3. ALIGNING _____

4. FIRING _____

"Leaders must wake people out of inertia. They must get people excited about something they've never seen before, something that does not yet exist."

Rosabeth Moss Kanter

INFLUENCE

Creating Faith

Should I have faith that you just picked up this book again after implementing an idea, action, or strategy from the last activity? As Leaders, when we ask our people to complete a task, if we have the right people, we can have faith that the task will be completed. Faith is a two-way street. Our people must have faith in us as leaders.

A primary aspect of leadership influence at any moment is faith. Faith itself is never absolute unless it is misguided. True faith is always relative. The sheer diversity of human abilities means that each leader will be trustable across certain domains and not others. At different stages of business growth and in different parts of the business, different leadership styles and leaders are needed. If you have read *The Strategy Book* to this point, you may see the value of the Strategic Mindset Process in one of two ways.

If you are a leader who is focussed on leading the future of your firm, the ideas you have jotted down on the blank pages, along with the questions, will all help. Your ability to cultivate a Strategic Mindset will be central to what you do. New value will come from sensing, seeing, connecting, planning, focusing, moving and then **repeating the six steps again and again**. If you are a leader focussed on managing the present, your written ideas will have more to do with your firm's current strategy and staying on track. Here, it will help to place *The Strategy Book* on your shelf and visit it periodically.

A leader who helped his people win was Lego Group CEO Jørgen Vig Knudstorp. The turnaround of the LEGO Group is one of the best customer and employee engagement stories in recent decades. Knudstorp shares that at LEGO[38], "Blame is not for failure. It is for failing to help or to ask for help."

Whether managing the present or helping to lead the future is more important, to implement strategy, a firm must build capabilities, create systems, and allocate resources to support their Strategy. Leaders must communicate the direction, perhaps via a Mission Statement or Mantra, hire the best people and train them to build the needed capabilities. When examining our ability to influence others, in my experience this comes down to the degree of trust, quiet confidence, determination and expertise we impart as a leader.

There are foundational elements to gaining basic trust. These include humility, vulnerability, and honesty. Nobody enjoys having a 'show off' for a boss unless the boss can learn to laugh at themselves. When it comes to honesty, subliminally, we can all sense a liar. Honest leaders can be scarce at times, and dishonest leaders can often become powerful influencers, for a time. We like honest people, and down the line, their potential to influence us is more significant.

Quiet confidence comes down to belief. If we genuinely believe the strategic direction being taken is right and that we can get things done, our faith grows. Overconfidence is the opposite of humility. If you are unaware of the Dunning Kruger Effect[39], please read the Endnotes section at the end of this book. Staying curious and seeking genuine regular feedback from colleagues that are aware helps to grow leadership confidence and faithful followers. Quiet confidence is also the product of discipline. Sometimes the most confident and capable organizational leaders are ex-military or have cultivated discipline in martial arts.

Determination in a leader can galvanize followers. In 1519, when military leader Hernán Cortés burnt all the ships, his men understood they would either win or perish. Cortés' ongoing strategic intent was clear to all. With no exit option, they stepped up and conquered the Aztec Empire. During the battles for Empires, armies would often besiege cities from three sides only, leaving open the possibility of escape. These cities invariably fell, as city defenders did not step up with full intensity to fight. Resilient and courageous Kimberly Clark CEO, Darwin Smith was ridiculed by the media when he led the sale of the company's paper mills to migrate forward in the Value Chain. Kimberly Clark's new Kleenex and Huggies brands ultimately outperformed Procter & Gamble in the market. Phrases like 'burn the boats', 'sink the ships' and 'sell the mills' are now common phrases for determined leaders.

Expertise is needed to lead and influence others. The type of expertise needed will vary as a business grows. The ability to identify and seize opportunities will be key during the start-up phase or within an R&D division. A little later on or higher up, expertise in enabling others becomes important. Once a business is mature, leaders will need expertise in big picture thinking and changing the organisational culture, systems, structure, and re-allocation of resources. Leaders who are experts embody expert authority. Authoritative leaders are honest, ethical experts who keep learning. Once the future target has been chosen, authoritative leaders, who are experts in the industry, customer, product, processes and their people, may only have to say, 'follow me.'

ACTIVITY 6.3
STRATEGIC LEADERSHIP

1. On the blank pages opposite, write the phrases, **'trust', 'quiet confidence', 'determination'** and **'expertise'**. For each, jot down three things you could do to be better in building faith in you as an honest, ethical and expert leader?

2. Show your list to a peer or colleague. Ask for their honest, **no holds barred feedback**. Repeat this exercise with two other people. Be strategic about it. Where do you lack the necessary expertise? What could you do differently to better lead your firm's or division's strategy and influence your people to deliver on it? Leaders come in all shapes and sizes. Each is wired differently. Paradoxically, a determined risk-taking entrepreneur may never engender quiet confidence in their people, no matter how much they work on it.

3. What could 'burning the boats' or 'selling the mills' look like for your business moving forward? **Communicating strategic intent clearly** and **aligning staff with it** are two of the most important tasks for a leader. As a leader, how regularly do you

communicate, convey, and articulate the Strategy? It is also important for competitors to hear your speech on strategy and the sorts of trade-offs you are making. When a competitor understands what your firm is committed to, they will be more likely to do something else, rather than copy, compete head to head and create a price war. When a leader cannot speak directly with employees, a strategy note may help. *The Strategy Note* is the title of my second book on strategy and it helps leaders with a strategic mindset to cultivate the discipline of the one-page strategy note.

4. Reflect on your people. When employees understand the Mission, they can help work out how to deliver it. **Employees** are people with a voice and a soul, that like fair processes and like to make a real and meaningful difference in their lives and the world. When employees help one another, a lot more of what needs to be done gets done a lot faster. Employees must ask for help when needed and be willing to help each other out. In consultation with your entire team, come up with agreed ways to reprimand and correct those who, act unethically, fail to help, or fail to ask for help. Healthy organizational cultures are not an accident. Unhealthy organizational cultures pose huge risks to a firm's strategic success. When people feel cared for and they care about what they do, firms thrive.

TRUST	QUIET CONFIDENCE
DETERMINATION	EXPERTISE

COMMUNICATE STRATEGIC INTENT

ALIGN PEOPLE WITH STRATEGY

"Technology is nothing. What's important is that you have a faith in people, that they're basically good and smart, and if you give them tools, they'll do wonderful things with them."

Steve Jobs

FUTURE-PROOF
YOUR BUSINESS

SIX
QUESTIONS

I created the term Strategic IQ to help future-proof your business and identify the areas within your firm's business planning processes which may need improvement.

Question 1. How well does your firm sense its outer business environment?

Please give your firm a mark out of 10.

Question 2. How well does your firm look ahead in time?

A. We don't look ahead very often.
B. We see 12 months ahead.
C. We see 3 to 5 years ahead.
D. We look 10 years ahead.

Question 3. Leaders in our firm

A. Seem out of touch with people and real issues.

B. Connect well with customers and employees alike.

C. Consult widely when formulating strategy.

D. Consult widely when formulating and executing strategy.

Question 4. In terms of creativity, over the last year, our firm has

A. not changed its strategy at all.

B. found ways to get even closer to customers and buyers.

C. introduced even better products/services or entered a brand-new market.

D. redefined the entire notion of value in our industry.

Question 5. When it comes to staying focused, we

A. most often feel lost.

B. are often distracted.

C. get the important stuff done.

D. have a team with lasers shooting from their eyes.

Question 6. When implementing a new strategy, we

A. struggle.

B. drag our feet sometimes.

C. always deliver projects on time.

D. love the pace of change and are proactive.

STRATEGIC IQ

YOUR STRATEGIC IQ SCORE

For Q1. Your score is the number you gave between 1 and 10.
For Q2. through Q6. Your scores are A= 1; B = 4; C= 7; D=10.

Calculate your Strategic IQ = (Scores for Q1 + Q2 + Q3 + Q4 + Q5 + Q6) =?

Interpreting your Strategic IQ Score

Under 20: This book could be your firm's wake-up call
20 to 29: There is still lots of room for improvement
30 to 39: This book can help you get smarter or *faster* or more creative
40 to 49: Your firm is an inspiration to others
Above 50: You can safely give this book to someone else

Review the questions you scored lowest on. Investing time, resources and effort in these areas will help future-proof your business the most.

CONCLUSION

At this moment, you and others reading this book will be in one of 193 countries around the globe, or you may be switching between countries via boat or plane, outside the exclusive economic zone of any country. If you purchased this as an audiobook or e-book, you might have downloaded it via the Internet from the World's largest data center – the Citadel. A *Critical Success Factor* in most industries, including the Data Storage Industry, is an ability to scale. At the time of writing, the Citadel is a 17.4 million square foot mega-facility in the wide-open spaces of Nevada, with plans to build three additional centres across the United States. The Citadel's *Claim to Fame* includes being powered exclusively by renewable energy. The Citadel's **domain** is global. The Citadel's objective includes cloud computing and is a powerful example of Michael Porter's concept of Horizontal Integration. The Citadel's *unfair advantage* is that it enjoys breath-taking snowy mountain views and equally breath-taking economies of scale, along with access to some of the world's most creative minds, both onsite and from nearby Silicon Valley, who help the Citadel's parent company triangulate real-world decisions.

The *Industry Attractiveness* of the Data Storage Industry the Citadel operates within is moderate, with no real substitutes. There are moderate barriers to entry in cost and regulatory approvals, so the threat of new entrants is moderate. The bargaining power of both suppliers and customers is moderate. The degree of competitive rivalry appears moderate to high. Benefits from complementary players should only increase with time. So, in summary, the Citadel enjoys a *Bluish Ocean* with gradually deteriorating conditions. This means Value Exploration should be a priority. Regardless of the forces at work, knowing the attractiveness of your industry should always be a priority for your business.

The Citadel is the *Core Business* of a company called Switch. Rob Roy, Switch Founder, has a Vision that includes the BHAG-like *Mantra* of 'Powering the Future of the Connected World' with a set of values that includes cultivating a unique client-oriented culture at every level of the company. Rather than over-relying on his status or charisma, Rob Roy appears to embody trust, quiet confidence, determination and expertise. Rob believes in his people, *communicates strategy clearly* and *aligns people with it*.

Under Rob's leadership, Switch has embraced a culture of diversity and equality and is a technology company where women represent more than half of its senior leadership team. The leadership team's motivation and drive aim to produce the absolute best results for clients with unparalleled client value and the data storage centre industry's best customer service. Switch understands the global forces at work, that many have been slower to appreciate. Switch **Sensed the Environment** and **Saw Beyond the Next Horizon** to jump in early and scale the Citadel quickly.

On the same site as the Citadel, Switch has placed bets and hedged against any weaknesses in their Strategy by co-creating an Innovation Ecosystem. In the Ecosystem, creative collaboration takes place between students, entrepreneurs, businesses, investors and non-profits, some of which are competitors, who end up co-operating in select parts of their respective *Value Chains*. The Citadel is also home to the Nevada Advanced Autonomous Systems Innovation Center (NAASIC), funded by the Governor's Office of Economic Development. NAASIC hosts innovative programs to commercialise stationary robots, advanced manufacturing systems, unmanned aerial vehicles, autonomous cars, underwater robots, AI and the Internet of Things. Good strategy requires creativity and a willingness to learn from others.

Switch's ecosystem programs explore options, migrate opportunities and enhance value. The Innovation Ecosystem is a diverse, capability building and expert-driven hive of activity which **Connects with Customers and Stakeholders**; **Plans Future Value Chains, Creations and Combinations** and sells licenses for leading-edge technologies to the World. With over 500 IP patents issued or pending, Switch, like Virgin, has **Focussed on Chosen Targets** and are poised to **Move Faster with Influence.**

Switch appears to have been diligent, ethically driven and disciplined with their Strategy. Switch has applied the six steps of the Strategic Mindset Process to master their environment and *Future-proof their Businesses*. They operate in the intermediate stages of the various Value Chains they have assembled. Rather than being a business to retail customer (B2C) company, Switch is very much a business to business (B2B) globally focussed firm. Whether your business is B2C or B2B, your primary objective is to know as much as you can about the needs of your *Ideal Customer* and then align your business model and activities with them.

Within its B2B business model, Switch encompasses four approaches to strategy, which reveals their appreciation of both industry predictability and customer adaptability. Switch took a *Market Approach* in building the Citadel. Switch took a *Visionary Approach* in creating its Nevada based Innovation Ecosystem, which itself is home to numerous experts experimenting and exploring value with an *Agile Approach*. Finally, Switch's Commercialisation Division connects with a *Partnering Approach* to shape new AI, cognition and advanced automation standards to create new views of the future and migrate value into Switch's existing businesses.

At times, Switch is a premium Product Provider, leasing cloud space and persuading new customers by Selling the Benefits of their renewable energy and data security story. In other parts of the business where greater intimacy is needed, Switch engages in Two-Way Relationships and commitments to Alliance Partnerships within their Innovation Ecosystem. Like Switch, being prepared to switch your approach to strategy quickly and adopt different approaches to strategy across your different businesses to increase customer intimacy will likely enhance your firm's learning and success.

Fifty-thousand years ago, during the summertime, it is likely that our Homo-Sapien ancestors scaled the Italian Alps to a vista of breath-taking snowy mountain views. They kept moving forward to conquer Fred's species. Our ancestors then migrated further and populated the entire planet. Over the last fifty years, computers began populating our planet.

Today, technology and the Internet are a global phenomenon, affecting every aspect of our lives and businesses. The Age of Machines imagined in 1984 and 1999 with movies like 'The Terminator' and 'Bicentennial Man' has now arrived.

Advanced cognition systems have replaced lawyers within our justice systems while attack drones with facial recognition software are now in use. Our future seems breath-taking, yet volatile. The stories of Fred and companies like Switch help ground us and remind us that the six steps of the Strategic Mindset Process are important in understanding our environment, navigating **VUCA**, ensuring stability, and helping to create the industries of the future. I encourage you not to be overwhelmed by technology, but rather connect creatively with others around it, and **Create a Strategic Mindset** to future-proof your business and shape our brave new world for the better.

"Companies are communities. There is a spirit of working together. Communities are not a place where a few people allow themselves to be singled out as solely responsible for success."

Henry Mintzberg

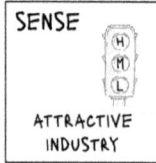

SENSE

ATTRACTIVE
INDUSTRY

CLAIM TO FAME

CRITICAL SUCCESS
FACTORS

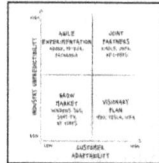

SEE

HORIZON ONE

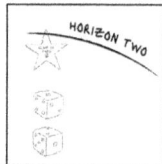

HORIZON TWO

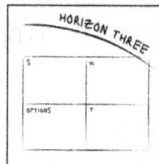

HORIZON THREE

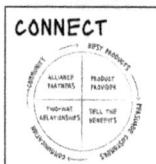

CONNECT

FIRST PRODUCTS

COMPETITOR

US   THEM

ORIENTATION

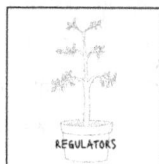

REGULATORS

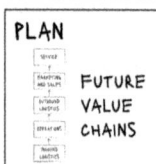

PLAN

FUTURE
VALUE
CHAINS

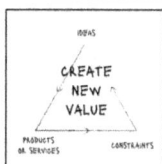

IDEAS

CREATE
NEW
VALUE

PRODUCTS
OR SERVICES   CONSTRAINTS

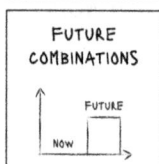

FUTURE
COMBINATIONS

FUTURE

NOW

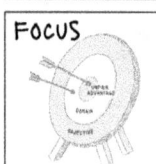

FOCUS

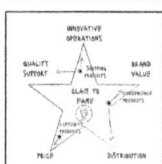

INNOVATIVE
OPERATIONS

QUALITY   BRAND
SUPPORT   VALUE

CLAIM TO
FAME

PRICE   DISTRIBUTION

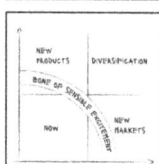

NEW
PRODUCTS   DIVERSIFICATION

NOW

NEW
MARKETS

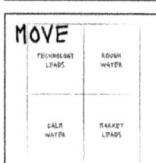

MOVE

TECHNOLOGY   ROUGH
LEADS   WATER

CALM   MARKET
WATER   LEADS

READY AIM

ALIGN FIRE

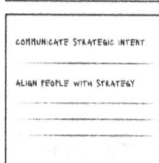

COMMUNICATE STRATEGIC INTENT

ALIGN PEOPLE WITH STRATEGY

ENDNOTES

INTRODUCTION

[1] **Mintzberg, Henry; Ahlstrand, Bruce; Lampel, Joseph** (1998). *Strategy Safari: A guided tour through the wilds of strategic management*, Free Press, New York.

CREATE A STRATEGIC MINDSET

[2] **Harari, Yuval Noah** (2014). *Sapiens: A Brief History of Humankind*. Vintage.

[3] **Pearce, Eiluned; Stringer, Chris; Dunbar, R** (2013). *New insights into differences in brain organization between Neanderthals and anatomically modern humans*. Proceedings Royal Society of Biological Sciences.

STEP ONE – SENSE THE ENVIRONMENT

[4] **Sinek, Simon** (2011). *Start with Why. How Great Leaders Inspire Everyone to Take Action*. Portfolio Books.

5 **Kim, W.C.; Mauborgne, R.** (2004). *Blue Ocean Strategy: How to Create Uncontested Market Spaces and Make the Competition Irrelevant.* Boston: Harvard Business School Press.

6 **Reeves, Martin; Hannaes, Knut; Sinha, Janmejava** (2015). *Your Strategy Needs a Strategy.* Harvard Business School Press.

7 **Magretta, Joan** (2012). *Understanding Michael Porter: The Essential Guide to Competition and Strategy.* Harvard Business School Press.

8 **Inc Magazine** (2015).

STEP TWO – SEE BEYOND THE NEXT HORIZON

9 **Taleb, Nassim** (2012). *Antifragile: Things That Gain From Disorder.* Penguin Books.

10 **McKinsey & Company, Inc** (2000). *McKinsey's Three Horizons of Growth.*

11 **Humphrey, Albert** (2005). *SWOT Analysis for Management Consulting.* Stanford Research Institute.

STEP THREE – CONNECT WITH CUSTOMERS AND STAKEHOLDERS

12 **Gladwell, Malcolm** (2000). *Outliers: The Story of Success.* New York: Little, Brown & Co.

13 **Walter Isaacson** *"The Real Leadership Lessons of Steve Jobs,"* Harvard Business Review, April 2012.

14 **Kahney, Leander** (2008). *Inside Steve's Brain.* London: Atlantic Books.

15 **Eden, Colin; Ackermann, Fran** (2011). *Making Strategy: The Journey of Strategic Management.* London: Sage.

16 **Hotelling, Harold** (1929), *Stability in Competition. Economic Journal.* Hotelling's Spatial Positioning Model describes stability in a marketplace

with a single dimension of competition, e.g., take-away ice creams, passenger flights, cellular network providers. A third player makes the system unstable unless each player is able to differentiate in some way e.g. flavours, different routes, network coverages.

17 **Paine, Lynn S**. *"Ethics: A Basic Framework."* Harvard Business School Background Note 307-059, 2006.

STEP FOUR – PLAN FUTURE VALUE

18 **Porter, Michael E.** (1985). *Competitive Advantage: Creating and Sustaining Superior Performance*. New York. Simon and Schuster.

19 **Carlopio, James**. (2010). *Strategy by Design. A Process of Strategy Innovation*. Palgrave Macmillan.

20 **Morgan, Adam; Barden, Mark.** (2015). *A Beautiful Constraint. How To Transform Your Limitations Into Advantages, and Why It's Everyone's Business*. Wiley & Sons.

21 **Brandenburger, Adam**. *"Strategy Needs Creativity."* Harvard Business Review, April 2019.

22 **Kim, W.C.; Mauborgne, R.** (2004). *Blue Ocean Strategy: How to Create Uncontested Market Spaces and Make the Competition Irrelevant*. Boston: Harvard Business School Press.

STEP FIVE – FOCUS ON A CHOSEN TARGET

23 **Corelli, Marie** (1905). *"The Spirit of Work"*. The Daily Mail. London.

24 **NASA Technology Transfer Program.**

25 **Collins, Jim; Porras, Jerry** (1994). *Built to Last: Successful Habits of Visionary Companies*. Harper Business.

[26] **Peale, Norman Vincent** (1963). *The Power of Positive Thinking.* Fawcett Crest.

[27] **IKEA Group.**

STEP SIX – MOVE FASTER WITH INFLUENCE

[28] **Luecke, Richard** (1994). *Scuttle Your Ships Before Advancing: Lessons from History on Leadership and Change for Today's Managers.* Oxford University Press.

[29] **Bruce, Robert** (2000). *Creating Your Strategic Future.* Harper Collins.

[30] **Welch, Jack** (2005). *Winning.* Harper Collins.

[31] **Slow-cycle markets** – markets where existing firms are shielded from competition for long periods because imitation is costly.

[32] **Standard-cycle markets** – markets where firms are moderately shielded from competition, because imitation is moderately costly. To remain sustainable, existing firms must keep increasing their competitive advantages.

[33] **Fast-cycle markets** – markets where firms are not shielded from imitation. 'Reverse engineering' of a firm's product or service by a competitor is common. Improving on the current offering is neither expensive nor difficult, due to the rate of change occurring in the market.

[34] **Switching costs** are the costs a customer incurs when they switch products or suppliers. Some switching costs are financial, opportunity or time-based. When switching between brands, there is often a psychological component, e.g., Some less expensive Japanese cars are as safe as more expensive German cars, yet many buyers will feel safer and more socially acceptable, driving a BMW.

[35] **Hamel, Gary; Prahalad, C.K.** (1996) *Competing for the Future*; Harvard Business School Press.

[36] **Bruce, Robert** (2000). *Creating Your Strategic Future.* Harper Collins.

[37] **Rumelt, Richard** (2011). *Good Strategy Bad Strategy: The Difference and Why It Matters.* Deckle Edge.

[38] **Boston Consulting Group** (2017). *An Interview with Jørgen Vig Knudstorp.*

[39] **The Dunning-Kruger Effect** is a cognitive error where people believe that they are smarter and more capable than they really are. Low ability leaders who enjoy early career success, due to luck, do not possess the skills needed to recognize their incompetence. The combination of poor awareness and low cognition means they overestimate their capabilities.

FUTURE-PROOF YOUR BUSINESS

[40] https://**www.switch.com**/

SKETCHES

1.1   Adapted from Michael Porter's Five Forces Model.

1.2   Inspired by Oscar Hauptman's Lectures in Operations Management.

1.3   Adapted from BCG's Strategy Palette.

2.1   Adapted from McKinsey & Company's Three Horizons Model.

2.2   Adapted from McKinsey & Company's Three Horizons Model.

2.3   Adapted from Albert Humphrey's SWOT Analysis Model.

3.1   Adapted from Robert Bruce's Wheel of Intimacy Model.

4.3   Adapted from W. Chan Kim and Renée Mauborgne's Four Actions Framework.

5.2   Inspired by Robert Bruce's Changing Customer Preferences Model.

5.3   Adapted from Igor Ansoff's Matrix and Robert Bruce's Zone of Sensible Excitement.

6.1   Adapted from Suarez Lanzolla's First Mover Advantage Matrix.

ACKNOWLEDGEMENTS

In his autobiography, Mark Twain wrote: "There is no such thing as a new idea. It is impossible. We simply take a lot of old ideas and put them into a sort of mental kaleidoscope. We give them a turn, and they make new and curious combinations. We keep on turning and making new combinations indefinitely, but they are the same old pieces of coloured glass that have been in use through all the ages." Some of my ideas for *The Strategy Book* came from another book entitled *The Idea Book*, which itself is a clever combination of two previously known things – a book and a notebook. I want to acknowledge fellow speaker, Fredrik Härén, who created *The Idea Book*. In the tradition of Mark Twain, Fredrik's humble formula for creativity involves taking a previously known thing and combining it with an idea in a new, unique and valuable way.

Isaac Newton, father of Mechanics, Universal Gravitation and the Laws of Motion once said humbly of his much smaller framed colleague, Robert Hooke, "If I have seen further, it is by standing on the shoulders of Giants!" I would echo this sentiment. Indeed, I have learnt a great deal about the art of strategy from many quarters. When it comes to the lion's share of inspiration for *The Strategy Book*, I would like to acknowledge the thought leadership of the Boston Consulting Group,

McKinsey & Company, Stanford Research Institute, Harvard Business School, Michael Porter, Henry Mintzberg, Nassim Nicholas Taleb, W. Chan Kim, Renée Mauborgne, Jim Collins, Adam Brandenburger, Richard Rumelt, Malcolm Gladwell, Fran Ackerman, James Carlopio and Robert Bruce. In memory, I am thankful to Steve Jobs, who offered the world so much as an innovative leader.

I am thankful to colleagues, mentors, friends and family for their willingness to read drafts of *The Strategy Book* and offer generous feedback: Rowan Gilmore, Oscar Hautpman, Fran Ackerman, Mario van Eck, Robert Bruce, Rebecca Hale, Lachlan Hale, Robert Hale and Jan Hale. Finally, I would like to thank my precious wife, Johanna Hale for her giant contribution to the creation of *The Strategy Book*. She read each draft to help enhance both message and meaning. Without her numerous shoulder rubs, delicious meals, timely cups of coffee and enthusiasm for my writing, this book would still be an idea.

ABOUT THE AUTHOR

John Hale is the founder of Hale Consulting Group, a globally focused management consulting firm specializing in strategy, people and change. As a keynote speaker, John has delivered over a thousand talks in twelve countries across four continents, to leaders from Fortune 500 and mid-sized companies to start-ups and public sector organizations. John has also worked as an early stage investor and advisor. He has been a Visiting and Adjunct Professor and has taught at various institutions, including Singapore Management University, Bond University and Melbourne Business School.

As a young child, John grew up in the developed and developing world. Living in both patriarchal and matrilineal cultures grounded him in the need for truth and justice as well as the ethics of care and co-operation. John brings a balance of sense and sensibility to his work. He currently lives in Australia with his wife and children.

HALE
CONSULTING GROUP
VALUE DRIVEN STRATEGIES

Hale Consulting Group is dedicated to helping organizations of all kinds drive value through better strategy, leadership and corporate wellbeing.

Please visit our website and explore

Keynote Speaking: John Hale shares value-driven ideas and strategies with thousands of leaders each year at global forums, national conferences and company events.

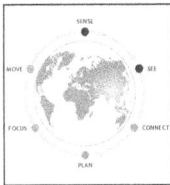

Consulting: HCG Consultants deliver strategy and organizational assignments for corporate, industry and professional groups, across a variety of industries in various parts of the globe.

Leadership Mentoring: HCG Consultants provide expert mentoring programs that empower leaders and help organizations advance in healthy ways.

www.halecg.com +61 407 301 200

www.ingramcontent.com/pod-product-compliance
Lightning Source LLC
Chambersburg PA
CBHW071558210326
41597CB00019B/3294